A Family Friend

BY THE SAME AUTHOR

CASEY WATSON

A Family Friend

**There was only one man
Sammy could turn to...**

This book is a work of non-fiction based on the author's experiences. In order to protect privacy, names, identifying characteristics, dialogue and details have been changed or reconstructed.

HarperElement
An imprint of HarperCollins*Publishers*
1 London Bridge Street
London SE1 9GF

www.harpercollins.co.uk

HarperCollins*Publishers*
Macken House, 39/40 Mayor Street Upper
Dublin 1, D01 C9W8, Ireland

First published by HarperElement 2025

1 3 5 7 9 10 8 6 4 2

© Casey Watson 2025

Casey Watson asserts the moral right to
be identified as the author of this work

A catalogue record of this book is
available from the British Library

PB ISBN 978-0-00-864172-6
EB ISBN 978-0-00-864173-3

Printed and bound in the USA

Dedication

I dedicate this book to all my readers who have ever been in care. It is not something we would wish for, but so often it's the only way. I know many of you had your lives transformed by a caring foster family, but some have had less positive experiences. I hope that you can find strength when looking back and continue to live happy and fulfilling lives, and that if you're ever in a dark place you'll reach out and talk to someone, because there is always somebody who wants to listen.

Sending love, Casey x

Acknowledgements

As ever, I have some important people to thank: my fabulous agent, Andrew Lownie, and the incredible team at HarperCollins, my publishing family, whose skill and expertise continue to bring these stories to you so brilliantly.

I must also give thanks to my friend and partner-in-writing-crime, Lynne Barrett-Lee. We've become such a team now that we can almost finish one another's sentences. And often do … when we're not busy writing, that is.

Once again, I cannot pass up the opportunity to thank my amazing family and friends, who continue to keep me sane, and support me in myriad ways. I simply could not do what I do without you.

Finally, I'd once again like to acknowledge all of you, my lovely readers. Your kind reviews really are all the encouragement I need to keep sharing stories of these so often forgotten children. You are the best. I send my love to you all.

Chapter 1

I've been in some locations and situations when I've missed fostering phone calls over the years, but whizzing down a hill with my little grandson on a giant plastic frisbee was definitely a first. So, when I felt my mobile phone start to vibrate in my pocket that morning, my first thought wasn't about whether it might get damaged – it was safely tucked away in an inside pocket, after all – but whether the caller would ever guess that my 'I can't answer right now' voice message was because I was out doing a bit of extreme sledging. I was, after all, fifty-seven.

But one thing was a given: I really couldn't answer. 'Hang on tight!' I told my grandson Carter. 'This could get messy!'

There are few things more guaranteed to bring a sense of joy and adventure than waking up to find the world blanketed in the white stuff, so I had already been feeling in the mood for some fun by the time my daughter Riley rang me on that otherwise ordinary Wednesday in January.

'All the local schools are closed,' she said, confirming what I'd already suspected. With a good few centimetres of the stuff having fallen overnight – way more than had been forecast – there was little doubt in my mind that today would be a snow day, not least because it was odds-on that half the teachers wouldn't have been able to get in to work. 'So, as you can imagine, Marley Mae's like a bottle of pop,' Riley added. 'And as Lauren has to work,' she said (Lauren being my daughter-in-law, my son Kieron's wife), 'I said I'd look after Dee Dee and Carter for her too. D'you fancy a couple of hours making snow angels and sledging?'

A couple of hours playing in the snow with my daughter and grandkids? Obviously, I didn't need asking twice. (Well, three of the five, anyway – Riley's boys, Levi and Jackson, the eldest of my grandchildren, were both now in high school and naturally had far cooler people to hang out with than their nana on a snow day.) So, it was a quick rummage for all the snow essentials – mittens, scarf, bobble hat, flasks of coffee and hot chocolate, extra socks, second and third pairs of mittens – and I was off in the car to meet them all at the park at the far end of town.

I knew half the local kids would be heading there too (not to mention any number of 'kidults' and parents) because it was the only place locally with a half-decent slope. In fact, once we'd scaled it, pulling the sledges

Riley had brought along, I realised it was a slightly steeper slope than I remembered from the last time we'd sledged, which must have been at least a couple of years pre-pandemic. Still, I thought, what was the worst that could happen? There was plenty of space at the bottom for crash-landings, so all I had to lose was my dignity. Plus, there were worse ways to be spending a weekday morning during what's traditionally the gloomiest time of the year.

For our family, it had been more than a little gloomy. My elderly parents' health had really deteriorated in recent months, particularly my mum's, following a nasty fall, and with Dad struggling to care for her, my sister Donna and I had been forced to make a pretty big decision: to persuade them to leave the home they'd lived in for decades and move to a flat in a supported living complex.

It hadn't been easy. Mum and Dad both cherished and valued their independence. But after months of planning and persuading, and a couple of difficult conversations, the previous weekend had finally seen them installed in a cosy ground-floor flat, which even came with a little patio that looked out over the communal gardens.

I couldn't begin to imagine how hard it must have been for them to leave the home they knew so well. And, as tends to happen in any life, as people become elderly and need to downsize, part company with so many of their possessions. That aspect had proven to be particularly vexatious. It wasn't the biggest of places, obviously, and though Mum and Dad had a lot more tolerance for clutter than I did, it was simply impossible for them to shoehorn in half the things they really felt they couldn't leave behind – not without having so much furniture in their living room and bedroom that they'd be constantly tripping over it. And more falls were the last thing any of us wanted. In fact, they'd dug their heels in to such an extent that there'd had to be a trade-off: they'd only countenance leaving stuff behind if I would accept being custodian, so I'd been forced to take boxes and boxes of stuff – old clothes and ornaments, books, crockery, vases, paintings and photos – as well as a few bits of furniture, even a load of art materials. My dad, always creative, had spent much of his early retirement dabbling in oil painting and the tools of his 'trade', plus the resulting works of art, filled a couple of large suitcases on their own. Not, I thought sadly, that he'd been able to do a lot lately.

But we'd got there, and now they were reassured that the belongings they loved but couldn't take with them hadn't ended up in recycling, we could only hope they'd adapt to their new, smaller living space and enjoy some happy years there together.

Right now, however, it was my own immediate future that was uppermost in my mind. This was our third run, but the confidence we'd gained from the first two was beginning to be offset by how busy the park was becoming. And as my mobile continued trilling, so too did

Carter with 'Watch out, Nana!', 'Mind that boy!' and other assorted anxious orders. This would, I decided, definitely be my last run of the morning. Well, if we made it to the bottom without colliding with anyone, that was.

Fortunately, some sixth sense made me lean in the right direction and though we tumbled off anyway, in an ungainly muddle of limbs, it was with whoops of laughter as opposed to yelps of pain. Ditto Riley, with the girls, all on the bigger, even faster sledge. Time for a hot drink and then the making of those promised snow angels.

But first, of course, I needed to check my phone. Because it was almost certainly Mum, Dad, or both of them together, calling about yet another vital task that needed to be dealt with immediately, or else life would become totally intolerable. So as soon as Carter had wriggled off my lap, I reached into my pocket for my phone. When I clicked to see who the missed call had been from, however, I was surprised to see it had been neither of my parents. It had been my supervising social worker, Christine Bolton.

This was unexpected. Christine and I had checked in just after Christmas and agreed that, for the moment, my husband Mike and I would be on a short 'sabbatical' so we could support my mum and dad. We'd also called a temporary halt on the intermittent respite work we'd been doing since our last long-term placement had finished the previous summer. We'd left it that I would get in touch with her again once my parents had been safely installed in their new place and have her put us back on her 'available' list.

So, was she psychic? I had literally only said to Mike that morning that I needed to put calling Christine on my to-do list. After so long concentrating on making sure my mum and dad were sorted, I was itching to get back to the day job; to have a new child in, and new fostering challenge, in my life. Waving my phone at Riley to indicate that I needed to make a call, I stepped away slightly from the melee of kids, mums, dads and grandparents, where the background noise would be a little less intrusive.

'Where on earth *are* you?' was Christine's first utterance when we connected, just as a whoop went up from another sledgeful of scattering children.

'Dicing with a broken bone,' I told her. 'I'm out having a snow day with Riley and the grandkids. How about you? Is everything okay there?'

'Oh yes, fine,' she said. 'Well, bar the fact that the heating's on the blink here and we're also three staff members down. I was just hoping for a quick chat about a child we need to place but it sounds like you have your hands full – would you prefer to talk later?'

'No, it's fine,' I said, watching Riley and the kids toiling back up the hill, 'and your ears must definitely have been burning.' I told her about the mental note I'd made that morning to call her. 'So, now's as good a time as any,' I went on. 'I'm grateful for the breather, to be honest. What's the story?'

'Well, first up, it's not an emergency or anything, though we'd obviously like to resolve it as soon as practical. Which is why I thought of you and Mike. I know you'll still have all sorts of things to sort out with your mum and dad so I absolutely don't want you to think I'm throwing you in the deep end, but I wanted to run it by you, just in case you might feel up for it. It's not a little one. It's a thirteen-year-old boy – name of Sammy – who's been in the system a long time already, so he would be moving on from another foster carer.'

'Why?' was the obvious question, so I asked it.

'In the here and now, according to his social worker, because he's not getting on with their son and doesn't want to live with them anymore. The boys had a fight a few days back – nothing major, just hurt pride and a few bruises from the sound of things – but though the carers have tried hard to get to the bottom of the argument and repair the relationship, Sammy's apparently made it clear he really can't bear to stay.'

'How old's their son?' I asked.

'Sixteen. And there's no previous to this, or so I'm told. I should say, by the way, that I don't know the case personally, or, indeed, the social worker involved – I've picked this up for someone else who's away – but she tells me that Sammy's been there for six months and everything's been fine up till now. By all accounts they've always got on well. So, it's probably something and nothing, but Sammy's adamant that he wants placing elsewhere. It's a great shame. There were apparently high hopes that he'd be settled there long-term ...' She sighed. 'For a change.'

My ears, toasty under my bobble hat, naturally pricked up. 'So, what's the background before this placement?' I asked. 'Have you had a chance to look at his files yet?'

'No, but I will, of course. All I know from Jen – that's his social worker – is that he's been in care since he was ten,' Christine explained. 'He entered the system after the death of his grandmother, who was his principal carer. It has all the markings of the usual sorry tale, sadly. Mum has spent most of his childhood thus far in and out of prison – more in than out, it seems – for offences involving drug dealing and prostitution.'

'Are they still in contact?'

'No. And not for a long time, I'm told. That ship's long sailed. I think the nan – the maternal grandmother – was very much the mother figure in his life and there are no siblings or other relatives. The only person he's stayed in touch with, and then only sporadically, according to Jen, is an elderly neighbour – a close friend of the grandmother. But he's apparently not in a position to help support the lad. Jen would obviously be able to tell you more, but since he came into care it's not been plain sailing. He's been passed around quite a bit, to be honest. Though, up until this point, it's been nothing to do with the lad himself, i.e. these moves haven't been due to any longstanding behavioural issues, just plain old bad luck. His first carers were new to the job and, after only six months, decided fostering wasn't for them; not because they didn't have the best intentions – simply that they found it too much of a tie. So, poor Sammy got moved on. The second set had a death in the family and needed some time out, so once again he had to be placed elsewhere. The third was a single female carer and when Sammy started acting out a bit following his move to a new secondary school, it all got too much for her. Again, there was nothing that would count as a red flag – she just had major second thoughts. Didn't feel she knew how to handle an adolescent boy and decided she would prefer to stick to girls anyway, so he had to be moved yet again. And so here we are, with him all settled in at – hang on, I can't read my own scribbles! – yes, at Sally and Eric Hawthorne's. And everyone thinking it was a really good fit. They're longstanding carers so their son is used to having other kids coming and going, but you know what it's like – teenage hormones and all that.'

I did indeed. I'd lived with my share of those, for sure, just as my daughter was doing with her teenage boys now. 'I hear you,' I said. 'And, oh, the poor lad. He must be feeling pretty unmoored and abandoned with all that re-locating, bless him.'

'Ah, so does that mean that you and Mike, at least in theory, might ...?' She let the sentence hang.

'Of course.' I told her about my mum and dad's move over the previous weekend. 'So, we're coming out the other side of all the stress now. Just crossing everything that they adjust to their new reality without too many hiccups. It's been a huge upheaval for them, obviously.'

I knew Christine understood. Prior to his death, she'd been through a very difficult period with her own father-in-law, who had been in denial about his worsening dementia. 'And a lot of stress for you as well,' she said, and not at all inaccurately. Though just knowing that if anything happened in the wee small hours they would now have a lifeline they could, literally, pull was a huge weight off my mind. Even greater than I'd expected. Knowing they were safe, and had that extra support network in place now, I was sleeping so much more soundly and that alone was making me feel a good deal better. Almost de-mob happy, if I was honest.

'And hopefully behind me,' I answered, feeling slightly guilty as I said it; perhaps 'de-mob happy' wasn't strictly appropriate. 'So, I don't see why not. It's just the two of us rattling around, after all. Let me speak to Mike tonight, though I'm sure he'll be happy for us to take the lad on. Can I call you back to confirm in the morning?'

'Absolutely,' Christine said. 'And there's no rush. I'm in a meeting till eleven. Just make sure you don't break any crucial bones in the meantime!'

Riley, by this time, had just finished another run with Carter while the girls had flown thrillingly solo.

'Nana? Or was it Grandad?' she asked as they all ambled over, her wry smile indicating how well she understood the strain I'd been feeling. I'd been chewing her ear off a fair bit the last few weeks and months. Persuading Mum and Dad that they had to move had been, of necessity, a whole-family campaign and Riley had been a huge support in getting them to accept it.

'Neither,' I said, putting my phone back in my pocket. 'It was Christine. She has a possible new long-term placement for us – a teenage boy.'

My daughter laughed. 'Oh dear,' she said. 'That's the rest of your day sorted then!'

I looked at her in confusion before the penny suddenly dropped. Both my empty bedrooms were, of course, currently occupied. With around five decades-worth of my parents' 'cannot possibly be parted with' possessions. Which would now, of course, need to be squeezed into one. Which was an impossibility. Plus, I needed *both* my empty bedrooms back, ideally, in case my son Ty and his girlfriend Naomi, currently living in York, came to stay. Which left precious few options and so would require a lot of sweet-talking.

'Oh dear' was about right …

Chapter 2

The following morning saw me in traditional whirling dervish fashion, dashing around the house in my marigolds and slippers, as I got everything ready for our new guest. And with the grandkids back in school now, the roads having been made passable, I'd also been able to rope Riley in to help me. She'd just left, after braving the still-freezing temperatures to transfer some of Mum and Dad's stuff into Mike's Man Cave (i.e. the garden shed) and some to her car. As well as getting his grudging permission to store some of the boxes in there, I'd also managed to twist my daughter's arm to take a few boxes off my hands on the understanding that it was *definitely* only temporary.

It still left me with a fair bit, but with a little ingenuity and a lot of humping and hauling on my part, I'd managed to find homes for it all. And having given a last belt-and-braces once-over to the bathroom, I felt satisfied that the house was squeaky clean. Just time for a quick coffee, then, and a mop of my sweaty brow before Sammy arrived.

He would be arriving a little sooner than had been intended. When I'd called Christine back the previous day to say Mike and I were both on board, the plan had been for Sammy's social worker to bring him to us in a couple of days, to give us time to do everything we needed to in preparation. All that had changed, though, just a couple of hours later. I'd been dishing up tea when another call from Christine came in.

'Could you perhaps take him sooner?' she asked. 'As in sometime tomorrow morning?' There had apparently been another nasty flare-up between the boys, she explained. 'And he's now threatening to self-harm,' she added, 'if we don't get him out of there.'

'Is there a history of that then?' I'd asked, alarm bells ringing slightly.

'No, not to my knowledge, but we obviously have to take him seriously. Jen's assured me that he's fine for tonight as the Hawthornes' son is on a sleepover with a friend, but if there's any chance she could bring him to you tomorrow …'

So, of course we said yes.

Sammy's social worker was called Jen Brown. As was the case with Christine, I'd not come across her personally, but I had heard the name and was reassured to find out that she'd been Sammy's social worker for almost all his time in care, because she would presumably have supported him through all his previous moves too. This one being his fourth, bless him. And every one of them going to live with complete strangers. And that didn't count him being taken into care in the first place, while grieving for the grandmother who, assuming I had the whole picture, represented the only family the poor child possessed. It was a stark reminder of just how traumatic a start in life he'd had. So, while having not had to go through several social workers wasn't much compared to the tragedy of his early life, that continuity was at least something to be grateful for.

Twenty minutes later, as I watched the pair both getting Sammy's belongings out of Jen's car, I felt even more reassured. It was obvious from their body language that they had a good rapport. I could hear her laughing at something he said as she handed him a bag, even at a distance and through the window.

Mentally crossing my fingers, I moved from my vantage point at the window in our little snug to go and greet them at the front door. With a service that was always on its knees and, in terms of staffing, a depressingly high turnover, not every child in care was so lucky. Fingers crossed Jen was in her job for the long term, because it was pleasing to get the impression that Sammy was in reasonably good spirits.

It was an impression that didn't change, either. I opened the front door and waved, and as I watched them walk down the path, it occurred to me that for a child who'd apparently been threatening to self-harm, his beaming smile seemed a little incongruous. But if there was one thing I knew about outward appearances it was that they could generally be relied upon to be deceptive. Most children learned to mask their emotions when they felt they needed to and, in my experience, those who'd been in care sometimes did so by default. Keeping emotions under wraps was a survival strategy for some kids and being guarded and unreachable was second nature to a few, particularly those who'd already suffered abuse or neglect. After all, if your trust in those around you had been destroyed, it made sense not to make yourself vulnerable.

I would take Sammy at face value, however.

'Welcome,' I said, holding out my hands to take some bags. Sammy clearly didn't travel lightly. Both he and Jen were heavily laden.

'Thanks,' said Jen, handing me a couple of bulging holdalls while Sammy, just behind her, lugged a brace of large rigid suitcases on wheels over the step. 'Our Sammy here has a bit of an online shopping habit, don't you?'

The boy in question pulled the sort of mock-exasperated face that made me think it was a conversation they'd had many times. 'Just as well I have a nice big empty wardrobe for you then, isn't it?' I told him, smiling. 'Anyway, I'm Casey. Come on in and get warm. It's Baltic out there.'

Not that Sammy seemed to be feeling it. While Jen, who I gauged to be in her early thirties, was wrapped up in one of those huge, almost floor-length puffa coats that were currently in fashion, Sammy seemed dressed for the summer. Having already taken in the bigger picture – a very slender lad, so much so that he looked as if a stiff breeze might blow him over, mid-brown shoulder-length hair, which was fine-textured, with a slight wave – I could, as he lined up all his bags by the staircase, now focus in on the details. He was wearing baggy, ripped jeans, with possibly more holes than denim, a skinny-fit white T-shirt under a light oatmeal-coloured jumper and with a daffodil-yellow knitted scarf around his neck. This, too, appeared to be more holes than wool and seemed to serve no practical use other than as a fashion statement. I also noticed that the jeans were rolled up at the bottom, making it hard to miss his skinny (and presumably very chilly) ankles and the extremely expensive-looking trainers on his feet.

Belatedly, I now realised that my expression might be giving me away because Jen grinned at me and said, 'Yes, I thought *exactly* the same as you when I picked him up this morning, but Sammy here doesn't feel the cold, do you, love? Well, at least he doesn't admit to feeling it. If it's a question of being warm versus being fashionable … eh, Sammy?'

'Fashion!' Sammy confirmed, his mouth widening into a grin, and with a theatrical flick of the yellow scarf around his neck. He had lovely eyes, I noticed. Long-lashed, with hazel irises which were flecked with a similar yellow.

'And you definitely look like a breath of spring air,' I told him, which caused his smile to widen further. 'Even if it is about one degree out there. Anyway, let me pop the kettle on and then we'll head on upstairs. I can show you your room and you can make a start on your unpacking while Jen and I sort out the paperwork. Plan? And what would you both like? Coffee? Tea? Hot chocolate?'

'Coffee, please,' Sammy said immediately. 'With oat milk. Do you have oat milk? Only it's just that I'm very slightly lactose intolerant.'

'Sammy, I'm not sure …' Jen started, but I waved a hand to stop her.

'Yes, I do indeed have oat milk,' I was able to reassure him. Though more from luck than meticulous planning as dairy allergies were usually detailed on the care plan, which I obviously hadn't seen yet. I only kept it because my eldest grandson, Levi, was also currently into it. Something to do with an environmental project he'd been involved in at school, during which they'd delved deeply into all things carbon footprint. Oat milk was, apparently, far better for the planet. So, I generally had a carton in the fridge, even if Mike refused to countenance having anything to do with it, because, he pointed out, 'Why would anyone want their coffee to taste of porridge?'

Sammy, clearly.

'Safe,' he said. 'And can I also use your loo? I'm proper busting!'

Having pointed Sammy in the direction of the downstairs loo, I took Jen into the main downstairs living area, where she took off her enormous coat while I filled and put on the kettle. 'He's quite the character,' I said.

'Oh, he's certainly that,' she agreed. 'And despite how this situation has come about, generally no trouble.' She placed her coat over one of the bar stools that ran along the side of our breakfast bar. 'So, fingers crossed, eh?'

'And you've not found out any more about what happened?'

She shook her head. 'And won't, I imagine. You know what teenage boys are like. Probably nothing, but in any case it'll be history for Sammy now. He's not one for opening up about much. He's a bit of a closed book, and to be honest I think he's …'

But the rest of our conversation would have to wait as we heard the cloakroom door close and moments later, he was back with us. I stored it away though. There was clearly more to know.

Since our son Tyler had moved away with his girlfriend Naomi – she was currently in uni – I'd always tried to keep his room free for their regular visits home. Tyler wasn't our actual son, but we had fostered him since the age of eleven and all loved him dearly. As far as we were concerned, he was a Watson, even if his surname said differently. And if it was hard to believe he had turned twenty-two now, it was harder still not to think of that room as his bedroom, what with all the posters and books and abandoned chargers, and other bits of teenage boy paraphernalia that remained there. But with the other room, the 'fostering one', often playing host to my younger grandkids, it had become crammed full of younger children's games and toys. So, once we'd cleared out Mum and Dad's stuff, we'd made the decision that, since our new guest was thirteen, it made a lot more sense to pack away all the personal bits that Tyler might want to keep and put Sammy in there instead. Plus, I had to be realistic. As time had gone on, and Tyler and Naomi had made friends in their new home city, those visits home were obviously less frequent. In fact, more often than not now, when we had some free time, Mike and I would travel to them instead. They had a perfectly good sofa bed after all and it was always fun to plan a mini-break to go and visit them.

'So, here we are then,' I told Sammy once the three of us had relocated all his stuff upstairs.

He clapped his hands together. 'This is sick!' was his immediate reaction.

'Isn't it?' Jen agreed. 'And wow, you were right about that wardrobe. It's enormous!'

'It's a bit of a family heirloom,' I said. 'It was originally my gran's. Anyway, why don't you make a start on getting yourself settled in while we do all the admin and then you can come down and join us for that coffee before Jen goes?'

He pulled a phone from his jeans pocket. 'Oh, and do you have the Wi-Fi code? It's just my followers will be dying to know where I've ended up this time.'

I quickly pulled out my phone so I could share the photo of the back of our router with him. I was a dab hand at this by now and knew that after arriving at a new place, the Wi-Fi code was the first thing most kids wanted these days. 'Followers, eh?' I remarked. 'Mister Popular, I presume?'

Sammy grinned as his phone pinged and he opened up the photo of the back of my Wi-Fi box. 'Thanks, Casey,' he said, though I wasn't sure if he was responding to the comment or the password. Perhaps it was both. 'And I'll save your number too, so we have each other's, and don't worry. I'll be posting lots of photos – mainly selfies, of course, but I know not to put your location out there. I'm very savvy,' he added, grinning again. 'Or so I'm told, anyway.'

Clearly. And, I thought, as Jen and I left him to it and headed back downstairs, quite unusual. Most kids cringed at the thought of parents – and foster parents – accessing their online adventures, yet here was this one, all over it, and so quick to reassure me that he already knew the drill. Savvy indeed.

Once we were back downstairs, Jen pulled out all the relevant paperwork. 'He's such a sweetie, Casey,' she said, smiling indulgently, 'I love him, honestly, and I'm sure you guys will too. It's just so sad that he's gone through all these moves, bless him. I'd hoped he would have been well settled by now.' She glanced up from the papers. 'Fingers crossed he has better luck with you, hey?'

I smiled rather than comment with promises I might not be able to keep and reached across to take the care plan she was holding out. It was just a two-page document these days, nothing like the reams of paperwork that used to accompany children back in the pre-internet age, but one that still had all of the important information on it. Last address, name of last carers, social worker, GP and birth parents. Usually just a paragraph or two about the actual child. This covered any behaviours, allergies, medication and, if I was lucky, a list of their likes and dislikes. In Sammy's case I learned only that his favourite meals were roast dinners and chicken curry, and that he seemed to be quite a solitary child, often preferring his own company in the confines of his bedroom rather than hitting the streets with friends. Nothing about any recent behaviours, though I guessed this care plan hadn't yet been updated to include any mention of the mysterious fight Sammy had had with his previous carers' son. Perhaps we'd get an update on that down the line.

'Seems straightforward,' I said, reaching for my pen to sign it at the bottom alongside Jen's signature. 'Though it doesn't say anything about his phone use or a safe care plan. Does he have one of those?'

A safe care plan often accompanied a child if there were any significant risks, to map out how to mitigate these and how to protect both ourselves and the child.

'No, he doesn't,' Jen said. 'I mean, considering what just happened at his last placement, we'd have done one if you'd had any other children in and of course when your manager calls, no doubt she will get one sorted anyway, just to cover your general house rules – dressing appropriately around others, not going into bedrooms uninvited, etc. – but as for anything in particular, then no, he's always kept hold of his phone. But you'll be reassured to hear, I'm sure, that he does seem to respect boundaries. He will usually turn it off at night if he has school the next day. Ideally, he would hand it over to be checked – he does use all the social media platforms, after all – but there's no chance of that. Teenagers, eh? Sure you know how difficult that would be!'

I did indeed. Crazy though it seemed to me, because I'd never allow it with my own kids and grandkids, I was powerless to insist that mobile phones be handed over, either for checking or for safe-keeping during the night. Yes, I could mitigate risks slightly by turning the Wi-Fi off at bedtime but as well as being a bit of an inconvenience for Mike and I, kids had ways around that – all it needed was someone willing to top up their credit, and with the cost of such things getting cheaper all the time, they could surf the Net as much as they liked.

And that was as much as I was going to learn that day, as it turned out, as Jen was in a tearing hurry. She had two important calls to make and little time left to make them. She was going away for a long weekend to celebrate a big anniversary. 'Any questions, though, do email. I'll pick them up first thing Monday. Oh, and I'll send through details about him going back to school as soon as the transport is sorted out. In the meantime, thanks *so* much for this, Casey,' she added as she shrugged her coat back on. 'It's such a relief to be able to go away, knowing he's settled somewhere.' She glanced around her. 'Specially somewhere as nice as here.'

'Not a problem,' I replied. 'Are you going anywhere nice?'

'D'you know what? I have no idea. My husband's booked everything.' Her eyes sparkled as she smiled. 'And I do love a mystery!'

Me too, I thought, as she went up to say goodbye to Sammy. Though when it came to our foster kids, only *so* much of a mystery. And at least it looked like our newest one wouldn't be particularly challenging on that front.

Well, I reminded myself, at least in theory.

Chapter 3

True to Jen's prediction, over the next couple of days, Sammy proved to be no trouble at all. He was unfailingly polite, and neat and tidy to a fault. By the time he went to bed on the Thursday evening he had already packed away all his stuff, and not just in the sense that he'd stuffed everything into drawers and cupboards. He was happy and seemed proud to show me everything he'd done, from creating a space on top of the chest of drawers to display all his toiletries, fragrances and jewellery to organising all his clothes, both in the drawers and the wardrobe, in such a way that it looked less average teenage boy's bedroom than the shop floor of a high-end boutique. This was clearly no stereotypical thirteen-year-old boy.

I was mindful, however, to keep Sammy's background in mind. Our last long-term placement, a girl of just six, had been similarly fastidious about her room. In her case, having lived most of her young life with a mentally ill mother, it had been all about having control over at least one aspect of her chaotic environment so I couldn't help but wonder. Did the same apply here? I guessed I would find out in time.

In one other big respect, however, Sammy *was* a stereotypical teenager, it having been clear from the get-go that he was almost surgically attached to his mobile phone, which accompanied him absolutely everywhere. Which obviously wasn't far, during that first forty-eight hours, since, having turned down an offer from Mike to accompany him to football ('I'm sorry, Mike, but I really don't *do* sport'), he didn't leave the house, preferring to catch up with all his 'followers' on his 'socials'. His phone really was his portal to the wider world.

So, it was definitely surprising, not to mention a little irritating, that, on the Sunday morning, I happened to be in the shower when the impossible happened: Sammy had been accidentally separated from his life-blood, which he'd left propped up against a cactus on the bathroom windowsill.

Naturally, since I wasn't looking for it, I had failed to notice it when I'd gone in there. I'd just been happy that the bathroom had finally been vacated. In fact, the first I'd known about it was when a rapping on the door started up, followed by urgent questions about the missing phone's possible whereabouts.

'Casey, please hurry up!' Sammy was pleading now, it having been established that it was indeed locked in the bathroom with me. 'I'm actually having a full-on panic attack out here!'

I sighed as I reached for my towel from the shower cubicle. I hadn't even had the chance to wash my hair yet.

'Okay, okay!' I called, as I wrapped the towel around me and dried my hands. 'Keep your hair on!'

So, I grabbed the phone, which, out of consideration for Mike and I, Sammy generally kept on silent. I already knew from glancing at the screen that he got so many notifications that, had he had the sound on, it would ping multiple times a minute, providing its familiar soundtrack to our modern lives. Was this the future? I wondered, as I padded to the door with the phone. That our real lives – in the here and now, in the actual physical world – would become so dominated by the incessant pinging of a trillion mobile phones, all of them demanding that we'd stop whatever we were doing and give them our immediate attention? I was still only getting my head around the fact that being an influencer wasn't a new fad anymore – nowadays it was the way many thousands of people went about making an actual, legitimate living. Like being a secretary, or working on an oil rig, or a hairdresser's, but with the service they provided being 'content' and if that content was deemed good enough, a load of devoted fans, which led to businesses climbing over one another to try and be the ones to get their 'endorsement' and shower them with gifts and riches. But I wasn't sure I'd ever really get my head around the idea that, instead of friends, young people seemed to hanker after 'followers'. It was something I saw with my own eyes all the time, as young people, and a fair number of older ones too, would try surreptitiously, and in some cases, completely unashamedly, to sneak a peek at their phones to find out what the ping meant in the middle of having *an actual real-life conversation*.

Still it was what it was and I guessed we'd work our way through the rules eventually. I also knew I had to try not to be a dinosaur. I opened the bathroom door just sufficiently that I could pass the phone through to Sammy. 'Here, Mr Popular,' I said. 'Disaster averted. Let's hope you haven't missed Armageddon or something.'

'Oh, thank you *so* much,' he said, sighing dramatically. 'I almost *died* when I couldn't find it. I thought I'd put it in my pocket, and then the door went and everything, and when I realised I hadn't, and that it wasn't in my bedroom ... Oh sorry,' he finished, presumably noticing the gimlet eye now staring at him through the slit between door and door jamb. 'What am I like?! *Sorry!* You go and finish your shower.'

I shook my head in bemusement after closing the door and stepped gratefully back into the embrace of the torrent of hot water. Which I could only hope would still be sufficient for my purposes. I *would* wash this straggly hair of mine no matter what the distractions. After all, with an image-obsessed thirteen-year-old now in the house, who knew when I'd get into the bathroom again?

Monday, at least, I reminded myself. As she'd promised, Jen had sent me an email on the Thursday evening to confirm what would be happening about Sammy's schooling and to pass on the good news that he'd be able to return to his current school.

Though it's actually a behaviour unit, attached to a big secondary school, she'd written. *An assessment unit, essentially, set apart from the main school buildings. Because of all his moves, and to be perfectly honest with you, Casey, a few behavioural issues, his education thus far has been a bit hit-and-miss. It took another downturn after he moved to his last carers, and rather than ending up potentially having to exclude him, they decided to pull him from mainstream classes and place him in the unit instead.*

I noted the 'to be perfectly honest with you' and the rather ominous 'a few behavioural issues'. But things coming to light after we'd taken a child on were pretty much par for the course, so I was used to it and it didn't worry me unduly. What kid in his situation wouldn't have a few behavioural issues, after all? I was mostly just glad he was in school, because that kind of routine, that social structure, was very important.

He attends three days a week, Jen had continued, *on a reduced timetable. A mix of the usual school subjects and with staff also working on his mental health – the idea being to work with him to improve his emotional wellbeing, and to build resilience, so he can hopefully go back to full-time attendance and return to the mainstream school setting.*

A Family Friend

So far, so straightforward, even if I didn't know what lay behind his part-time attendance. Whatever that had been, it seemed the intervention had been a very positive step. Jen went on to explain that they would review the situation at the end of the current school year, and if that didn't seem viable perhaps move him on to a specialist school. But that was for the future. In the meantime, re-commencing after the weekend, he was all set to start again, being picked up by a local taxi at 8 a.m. sharp, on Mondays, Wednesdays and Fridays. No, it wasn't ideal. He should ideally be attending school full time. But in straitened times, and with so many kids with a mental health flag now, he was lucky – you had to take what you could get.

In the meantime, I could only try to chip away, little by little, at what went on under Sammy's highly polished, and seemingly impermeable, veneer. Jen had been right about that too; in the last couple of days it had become increasingly obvious that he liked to operate in the here and now and only skate across the surface of his past. He was clearly highly averse to opening up about himself and had antennae that could pick up the slightest hint of an incoming personal question, not to mention a stock phrase to head it off as well; something that sounded as if it had been long rehearsed. Ask him the most innocuous thing related to his childhood, his feelings, his memories or his interests and you'd be shut down almost immediately with a pair of raised hands and a 'sorry, but I never, *ever* go there'.

Mike, as ever, had taken a 'let's wait and see' position. We weren't even a week down the line, after all. But he was, of course, busy with his work as a warehouse manager. I, on the other hand, felt the usual instinctive itch. And since we'd signed up for the long term, I felt it was important to get to know Sammy; how else could we support the work the teachers and counsellors were doing with him? So, although it would obviously be a softly-softly approach, I was keen to at least try and scratch that surface. And not least because in the brief time Sammy had lived at our house, no less than a dozen or so parcels had arrived with his name on. That online shopping habit Jen had mentioned was very real. And, by extension, so too must be the money to pay for it.

I decided to tackle him about it over breakfast. 'So, are we expecting anything else in the mail today?' I asked, nodding to the package he'd already opened – another pair of trainers, the delivery of which he'd temporarily abandoned his precious phone for.

'Erm, I don't think so,' he said, tucking into the sausages and fried eggs I'd cooked for him. 'But who knows?! Honestly, I lose track myself sometimes!' He rolled his eyes theatrically, but then laughed and looked across at me. 'What am I like?! That's a lie,' he said. 'I *always* know what's coming. I keep a list in my notes on my phone.'

He would probably need to. Starting pre-dawn on the Friday morning, and with the first parcel handed to Mike on his way out to work, the stream of deliveries hadn't stopped. There had been expensive men's cologne, a gold necklace, various face products and potions. Plus, other things that he'd taken straight up to his room while I'd been otherwise engaged for whatever reason. There was no secrecy, however. No sense of sneaking around. He bought stuff, it arrived, it just *was*.

How on *earth* was Sammy funding all this? It was something Jen could probably shed light on next week. Perhaps he'd had some kind of inheritance from his gran. But, me being me, I wanted to know *now*.

'Sweetie,' I said, 'those trainers look very posh. Where do you get the money to buy such fancy stuff?' There. I'd asked the question that had been constantly nagging at me over the last couple of days.

Sammy stopped eating again and then he shrugged. 'I just do. You can ask anyone. I've always had plenty of money and I'm careful with it, too. I have online banking on my phone so I can keep an eye on what I'm spending. I don't waste my money.' His tone was proud rather than defensive. 'I only buy stuff I need.'

A gold chain? Those very expensive trainers I was looking at? The ones on his feet and in the wardrobe? Hardly things a boy of his age actually needed. 'Fair enough,' I conceded, 'and that's good to hear. But where has all the money come from? Did you have a job or something before you came here?'

He licked some grease from a finger. 'Well, I did actually have a little job – delivering milk and eggs with a guy down the road from my last carers but one – but that was a year or so ago, before I got moved last. But yes, I did save my wages and topped up my savings with my pocket money.'

'Pocket money?' I asked, trying to keep my voice conversational. 'From your last foster carers?'

Sammy immediately shook his head. 'No. Well, yes, I did get an allowance. But no, I mean from my uncle. He always sends me money – you know – for Christmas, and Easter, and my birthday and everything.'

'Uncle?'

He nodded. 'Uncle Kenny. He says it's easier than buying me gifts I might not like, so I get that money, and that's quite a lot too.'

'Ah, I didn't realise you had an uncle,' I said, stopping short of asking another direct question. I was obviously keen now not to push this too far, despite my instinctive itch going crazy.

'He's not a proper uncle,' he said. 'You know, not an actual *uncle*-uncle.'

The penny dropped immediately. Could this be the elderly neighbour, the friend of Sammy's gran Jen had mentioned?

'Ah, so your old neighbour? Your gran's friend?' I asked lightly. 'That's nice,' I added quickly, 'that he still looks out for you like that.'

There was a pause. The subtle sense of the atmosphere shifting. I could tell Sammy wasn't sure where this chat of ours was going and I in turn wasn't sure whether to wait for a reply or change the subject. I opted for the latter but before I opened my mouth to speak, he'd already chosen. 'Can we not talk about this?' he asked, his voice a little plaintive. 'Only I really don't like talking about things like this. It upsets me.'

'Oh, goodness me, Sammy,' I said, 'the last thing I want is to upset you. I'm just interested, that's all. And of course it all makes sense now. Absolutely no need to talk about it anymore. But I'm glad for you. That you have your Uncle Kenny to help support you. Do you –'

He pushed his plate away, decisively. 'I'm finished,' he said. 'Thank you. Is it okay if I go up to my room now?'

'Yes, of course,' I reassured him. 'You do whatever you like, love. I'll be off shopping later, if you want to come with me? Around lunchtime, I imagine. Once I've finished my housework. I'll give you a knock, shall I?'

Sammy stood, picked his plate up and passed it across to me. 'Okay. And, look, I'm sorry,' he said, his expression now slightly sheepish. 'I know it sounds silly, but I don't, you know –' he paused for a second – 'really *do* these kinds of leading conversations. If, you know –' another pause, a wan smile '– if that's okay?'

Which, of course, it was, or would have to be. So, I nodded and agreed that yes, of course, it was okay, and as he walked off and headed back upstairs, phone and trainers both in hand, I reflected that that was me duly told. But 'leading conversations'? On the face of it, such an odd thing for a thirteen-year-old to say. Unless you were a child who had been a while in the system and for whom leading conversations would have been a regular fixture, as well-meaning professionals, intent on doing their best for you, probed and prodded to find out what made you tick.

And that now included me, of course. *Back off, Casey.* But it didn't take a rocket scientist to arrive at a theory. He was thirteen years old and there was a man in his life who was regularly giving him quite substantial sums of money. Yes, it might be completely innocent. I truly hoped it was. But there was no getting away from the fact that the idea of a kindly uncle was a personal red flag, especially when innocent enquiries provoked such a marked response. It was sad to even think about it, but I'd had numerous experiences of 'uncles' in our foster children's lives, almost all of which had been highly unsavoury. Drug dealers. Pimps. Sometimes both. To most people the idea is just too dark, too unthinkable a conclusion to immediately leap to, but unfortunately, I'd seen that side of life too many times to just accept what I was being told at face value.

There was also the small matter of how adept Sammy had been at navigating the conversation along the routes he wanted it to go, never mind me being the one 'leading' it. In fact, as I scraped the remains of his breakfast into the composting caddy, I got the distinct impression that I was being played at my own game.

But Jen would surely know more about Uncle Kenny, wouldn't she? And, I reassured myself, I probably *was* leaping to conclusions. After all, was it seriously likely that if 'Uncle Kenny' was *that* kind of uncle, social services wouldn't already know?

Chapter 4

When you take in a new foster child, one of the key meetings early on is a thing called the initial placement review. This is a chance for all involved parties to 'check in' and discuss things. To iron out any wrinkles, see how the child is settling in and generally make an informal plan going forwards. In our case, the involved parties were me, Jen and Christine, and, of course, as was normal procedure, the child in question, Sammy. Which is why I was a little taken aback, come the Monday afternoon, to hear Jen, after filling me in on her anniversary mini-break to Edinburgh, telling me that he wouldn't be involved.

'What?' I said. 'Why?'

'Because he never is,' she told me. 'So, since we're going for this coming Thursday, I'm arranging for an outreach worker to collect him and take him off out for a bit. In an ideal world, we'd have arranged it for one of his school days, obviously, but with everyone's diaries groaning ... sure you know how it is. Anyway –'

'But why?' I said again, as this was highly unusual. A child of Sammy's age would always be expected to attend these reviews. 'Surely he would want to be there, wouldn't he?'

'You'd think so, wouldn't you?' Jen agreed. 'But sadly, it's not the case. Though not because we haven't tried. And he did attend the first couple, to be fair. But after his second move, it became apparent that it was pointless insisting. He'd simply sit there in silence and refuse to engage. And it's fine,' she added. 'Really. There's nothing major to discuss, is there? Did he head off to school okay this morning, by the way?'

'He did indeed,' I said. 'In fact, he was so keen to get there that he was up, showered and fed a good half an hour before the taxi came.'

'That's good to hear,' Jen said. 'Probably excited at the prospect of reconnecting with his mates.'

'But, Jen,' I went on, 'there is something else I wanted to talk to you about. This Uncle Kenny character. Do you know a lot about him? Sammy tells me he regularly sends him money – quite a lot of it, I imagine, given the amount of stuff that he's already had delivered here. He's a former neighbour, right?'

'Yes. An old friend of Sammy's grandmother. Was quite a key figure in Sammy's life when he was still living with his mum. Used to babysit regularly, specially once the nan became Sammy's principal carer. He's not family, of course, but he's still very much a grandfather figure. Why? Has Sammy said something?'

'No. Only that he sends him money for birthdays and Christmas and so on. Does he see him at all?'

'No. Well, not as far as I know. It's never been practical. He's always been placed with families that live too far away.'

'And he's never asked to?'

'No. They just keep in touch on WhatsApp. To be honest with you, I think it's one of those situations where Sammy's quite happy with things as they are.' She chuckled. 'You know what teenagers are like. I suspect he quite likes the arrangement as it is. And if the old guy gets pleasure from helping Sammy out, where's the harm? I don't think he has any family of his own to spend it on.'

I knew Jen's matter-of-fact appraisal of the situation should have reassured me, but it didn't, though I stopped short of suggesting there might be other, darker motivations. She knew the boy, and the background, much better than I did. And besides, she quickly followed that by making her apologies, saying she had another meeting to rush off to.

'So, we'll be with you around ten on Thursday, if that works for you? Someone will be along to collect Sammy just before that.'

'But if he decides he does want to attend? I'll call and let you know, shall I?'

'Yes, of course,' she said. 'But trust me, he won't.'

* * *

'Another thing he doesn't "do", then?' Mike observed on Thursday morning. 'Perhaps we should compile a list and stick it up on the fridge!'

It was early, still dark, and he was finishing his coffee. Early days, I thought, noting the slight irritation in my husband's voice. With him at work most of the time, and Sammy so often holed up in his room, I knew it would take time for their relationship to develop.

Though it hadn't snowed again, it had been another bitterly cold week. And a quiet one; bar the daily parcel arrivals, and Sammy's two days back in school, it had been pretty much like weekdays in January tended to be. A bit dull, a bit gloomy, a bit too far away from spring still. Though there had at least been one heartening exchange. When Sammy arrived home from school the previous afternoon and began sorting out his bag, I noticed and remarked upon the cover of a big sketch book he'd brought home with him, which was minutely decorated with line drawings and doodles.

'Did you do all this?' I asked, impressed by his evident talent.

'Course,' he said. 'We're allowed to,' he added quickly, obviously fearing I'd tell him off. 'Some people cover their books with collages and stuff but I really like drawing. Have a look, if you want. I'm working on some ideas for a big art project we're doing, to go up in the school hall.'

So, I'd picked up the book and fanned through the pages, the first few of which were a riot of sketches and studies, all nature-based and clearly destined for a bigger work.

'It's going to be about re-wilding,' Sammy explained, 'and Mr Donaldson says I can have a whole A2 space in it, *all* to myself.'

'I'm not surprised,' I said. 'You're a talented artist, love, for sure.'

He beamed. 'Mr Donaldson said I might even be able to take an art GCSE early.'

'Really?' I said. 'That's amazing!'

But the glow that had come from that small positive exchange quickly faded because shortly afterwards, just as Jen had predicted, Sammy's response to my question about whether he'd like to attend his own review meeting had been pretty much that – that he didn't 'do' meetings with social workers, because, like, what was the point? What difference would it make, him being there? And when I pressed a little, suggesting he might like to have some input, into what he was happy about, for instance, about anything he might not be, he'd looked at me as if I'd recently been teleported down from Mars. 'Why?' he'd argued. 'When I can just say all that to you anyway?' To which I really hadn't had much of an answer.

'Perhaps we should make a list,' I agreed, as I made my husband's lunch. 'Only I imagine it wouldn't take long till we needed a bigger fridge.'

Mike drained his coffee and nodded towards the back door. 'To go with the bigger cardboard recycling bin!'

he quipped. 'Still, there are worse problems to have, eh? So why run around trying to create them?'

He was right, of course. Much as I trusted my hunches, things were no doubt exactly as Jen had explained. That Uncle Kenny was the kindly old neighbour she'd described, who still kept in touch, much like any other elderly relative, doing the modern-day equivalent of sellotaping a ten-pound note to a grateful child's birthday card. Yet the way Sammy had shut me down so comprehensively still bothered me. If that was the case – especially given that he'd been so frank about Kenny's largesse – why had he then been so quick to clam up about him?

It was with that niggle still in mind that I waved Sammy off with his outreach worker (a young guy called James, who was going to take Sammy to the big, out-of-town shopping mall – no surprises there) and did a quick tidy-up before the meeting. So, when I saw Christine and Jen getting out of Jen's car, it was my first thought when I saw their expressions. It was all too obvious: something was up.

It would be great at this point to be able to report that my questions to Jen a few days earlier had borne investigative fruit; that my trusted instincts had opened a Pandora's box. In reality, it would turn out I deserved no such credit.

For now, though, I only knew that *something* had been going on. 'Everything okay?' I asked Christine as she led the way, stony-faced, up my front path.

'Er, not exactly,' she said. 'There's been a development.'

Since there was little point in going through the usual bullet-pointed agenda, I made everyone drinks, got the biscuits out and settled down to hear what revelations were about to be shared. And though Christine led the meeting, she handed the reins straight to Jen.

'You must be psychic,' she told me, 'because only an hour or so after we spoke on Monday, I got an email from the Hawthornes, asking if they could talk to me urgently. Their son had apparently got some things he wanted to tell us. So, I drove to theirs on Tuesday – better for the lad than dragging him along to the office – and he told us what his fight with Sammy had actually been about.'

'Uncle Kenny?' I asked.

Jen shook her head. 'No. Well, yes, potentially. And I'll come to that but, no. He just came forward because he thought he should do the right thing, had been agonising over it since Sammy left. It seems he'd overheard a phone conversation that he thought sounded "a bit dodgy" – his words – between Sammy and someone the lad got the impression was trying to do some sort of deal with him. He thought it was drugs. As you would. And since his mum and dad were out, he decided to confront Sammy, rightly furious to think this foster kid was dealing drugs in his mum and dad's house. They ended up fighting, as you know, and then we had the whole situation with Sammy insisting he couldn't stay with the Hawthornes – and to be honest, the Hawthorne boy was just glad Sammy had left.'

'But he never told anyone what they'd been fighting about?'

'No, because he didn't have any proof and he was also worried about the consequences if he did. He was – ahem – between us – not averse to smoking the odd spliff. He just thought it best to let sleeping dogs lie. Which he did, for a bit, but as the days went on, he began thinking it all through and reaching a different conclusion. Sammy had apparently been furious at the accusation that he'd deal drugs in their house – properly mad about it. And when he went back over the snippets of conversation he'd heard, he kept coming back to the word "files", which made him wonder if it wasn't drugs after all. Anyway, long story short, he told his mum and dad and they came to us.'

'And you put two and two together?'

'Not us,' Christine said. 'The Hawthornes did. They obviously knew about "Uncle" Kenny and the role he'd played in Sammy's life – it's never been a secret, has it, Jen?'

'No, not at all,' she confirmed. 'And it seems their lad had something else to disclose; he was pretty sure that Sammy had gone to visit him at least once in the time he'd been with them. Not through any official channel obviously, or I would have known about it – excuse me while I blush – but there were a couple of incidences when Sammy was supposed to be at some afterschool club but hadn't been and the Hawthorne boy's sure he'd gone over to the part of town where he knew Sammy had come from, because he found a train ticket. He says he did ask him about it and Sammy begged him not to tell on him; said he was just seeing a friend he'd made from his previous foster placement and that he didn't want to get into trouble at school and – smart, this – "make any trouble for the family".'

Jen paused to sip her coffee. 'So, that's what we started with,' Christine said. 'And as you know, I haven't been involved in this case so I thought I'd better do a bit of digging. You know pretty much the same as I do, but one thing that's turned up is that when the nan died, this Kenny character actually offered to take Sammy in. He'd known the boy all his life and they were obviously very close, but as he wasn't a blood relative, it was explained to him that the only way he could do that would be to go through the usual procedures and be properly assessed. He then withdrew the offer – said he was too old to bother with all that at his time of life, so in the end Sammy was placed in care instead. And since then, as you know, they have remained in touch.'

'So, you think maybe he decided not to go through the process because he knew something bad might show up?'

'We can't know that, obviously,' Christine said, 'but it would certainly be a motive to do so, wouldn't it?

Though it obviously doesn't tie him directly with what's been reported by the Hawthornes' son.'

'So, what does?' I asked. 'Anything?'

'It was all supposition at that point but, given that we knew there was regular phone contact between them, the logical next step was to request a police check, as you'd do with anyone in regular contact with a child in care. And it turned out that "Uncle" Kenny has a criminal record.' She paused. 'For distributing indecent images of children.'

'Files,' I said, half to myself, my brain whirring. Hadn't the word 'files' had been mentioned? I looked at them both. 'But what are the implications? Surely where the Hawthorne boy's disclosures are concerned – where *Sammy* is concerned – this is all still supposition?'

'It is,' Christine agreed.

'But it does explain why Sammy went all peculiar on me,' I said, 'when I asked him about his relationship with the man.'

'Exactly,' said Jen. 'I think Christine and I are of a mind here – that Sammy concocted all the stuff about not being able to bear living with the Hawthornes anymore not because he was in terrible distress but because he was anxious their son had found something out that he really, really didn't want found out – and that he might soon dig for more. My hunch is that he wanted a fresh start so he was out from under the lad's radar.'

'And of course he knows how to play the system,' Christine added.

And me, I thought.

'Wow,' I said, 'this isn't quite the review I was expecting.' I proffered the biscuits and both of them took one.

'I *know*.' Christine said. 'T'was ever thus, eh? What a week! But all credit to the Hawthorne boy for coming forward and alerting us to all this.'

'You're telling me,' I said. 'Whatever "this" turns out to be. So, what happens now?'

'Well, given that he has a criminal record, Uncle Kenny must now be added to the risk assessment at this review and Sammy has to agree not to go anywhere near him. I'm so sorry, Casey – this has somewhat put the cat among the pigeons for you, I know. Does this affect things for you going forwards? This placement is obviously a lot more complicated than I realised.'

I thought for a moment. Was she worried that I might want to pull out now? Should I? I wondered what Mike would say.

But I already knew what he would say. That we'd committed to the lad now and the fact that the circumstances weren't quite as first billed – that, potentially, they were much more challenging – made no difference. In fact, if Sammy was deeply embroiled with the sort of character no one would like to meet down a dark alley, that was all the more reason to try and support him in escaping from his clutches.

'Not at all,' I reassured Christine. 'Nothing changes.'

Which left just one elephant in the room to discuss. The fact that Sammy, out shopping, and oblivious to these revelations, would now have to be told, without delay. And, as per protocol, the person to do it would be his social worker.

I looked across at Jen and frowned, and could see her read my thoughts.

'You're right, Casey. I am definitely *not* looking forward to it.'

Chapter 5

My heart sank as I waved off my visitors. This must surely be the worst placement plan ever! Because that's what it felt like. I'd sat through many over the years and though almost all tended to throw up obstacles and new information about a particular child's behaviour, I couldn't recall ever taking on a child under one set of circumstances, only to find that the placement I'd agreed to was going to be a completely different thing. This clearly wasn't simply a young boy who had been moved around the system a few times in need of a stable home, there were obviously lots of other things going on – and had been for some time, it looked like. His was a past, it seemed, shrouded in secrets.

This wasn't the first time I'd encountered something that appeared to be 'seedy' either. It hadn't been that long ago that we'd looked after a teenage girl who'd had a whole cottage industry providing phone sex for clients. They were actually paying her to talk dirty and to pleasure herself as they watched. It was horrific, and all going on under my roof, in my own back bedroom! Luckily, having found out about it, I'd been able to put an abrupt end to the whole sordid thing, but it was territory I really didn't want to revisit.

Yet it seemed I was going to have to do exactly that. Still, I thought, as I watched the car disappear down the street, I should at least thank my lucky stars that I wasn't the one who was going to have to tackle Sammy about it all. The task would fall to poor Jen and time was obviously of the essence. So, since Sammy was in school tomorrow, we'd arranged that she'd pop back then, at around five, once he'd been dropped back home. All I had to do was break the news to the boy that a) he had to see his social worker the next day and b) this time it was non-negotiable.

It wasn't long before Sammy and his outreach worker James pulled up outside, in the same snazzy red Mini they had set off in. I smiled as I watched James climb out of the driver's side. He was over six feet tall and once he was upright beside it, the car looked almost like a toy. I couldn't imagine he was comfortable in it, so it was an interesting choice.

I also experienced my usual curiosity about why he was doing the specific job he did. Social services, career-wise, was a very broad church. At the centre of it, and the job everyone has usually heard of, is the social worker, obviously. But there are so many other roles and career paths to choose from – foster carers, like

Mike and I, child psychologists, play therapists, and so on, as well as the obligatory several layers of management. Becoming an outreach worker, fulfilling the sort of duties James was doing now, was very much a 'try before you buy' kind of option, since you could get into it without first following a higher education pathway and could experience the reality of work in the sector before fully committing to it as a career. You could also generally work your way up some distance – eventually becoming, say, a children's home manager – or decide if you wanted to go all in and study for a degree in social work.

Another group who often took on outreach work were the classic empty-nesters – people who had always been interested in working with children, or other vulnerable groups, and who, with their own kids flown from the family home, were now finally able to do so.

James, however, was definitely in the first camp. As I watched him helping Sammy pull his stash of carrier bags from the back seat, I suspected he was probably no older than early twenties himself. *Good*, I thought. A young male adult in Sammy's life could only be a bonus, so I crossed my fingers that we'd be seeing more of him.

They rattled up my path side by side and their body language was certainly telling; while I'd been plumbing the depths of potential depravity with my similarly careworn colleagues, these two looked as if they'd had a high old time. And Sammy was clearly keen to press on and re-inspect all his purchases. With a quick high-five and a 'laters!', directed at James, he shuffled past me and headed straight on upstairs with his haul.

'Yes, I had a lovely time, thank you, Casey,' I said, rolling my eyes.

James grinned. We obviously both knew what thirteen-year-old boys could be like and I wasn't about to burst Sammy's bubble. That necessary fly in the harmony ointment could wait till later. 'Do you have time for a tea or coffee?' I added. 'I've just boiled the kettle.'

He shook his head. 'Thanks, but 'fraid not. I've got a meeting to get to. Plus, we've not long had one; had to stop at a drive-thru because, and I quote, Sammy would "totally die of starvation" if I didn't.'

I laughed and then thanked him for his time before heading straight up the stairs so I could have a nosey at what the boy had brought home. Being something of a professional shopper myself, I was always excited to see the contents of other people's shopping bags, especially the designer ones that Sammy had returned with.

I sat down on the bed. 'Come on then,' I said, putting the events of the meeting firmly out of my mind for the present, 'let's see what you got. I bet you're dying to try it all on.'

Sammy grinned at me, completely guileless. He had the loveliest smile and I had to push down hard on the unsavoury by-product that came with that thought. 'You already know me so well, Casey!' he exclaimed, clapping his hands together. And, right on form, dived straight on in to show me his treasures. Designer sunglasses came first. 'Don't actually need the sun to look good,' he said as he put them on. 'So, what do you think?' he asked, pouting for good measure.

'Oh, very Kardashian,' I said. 'And seriously, they really suit you. Anyway, what else do you have here?' I added, reaching over to the nearest carrier, him having been side-tracked by pulling selfie-faces in the mirror.

'Hey, wait!' he said, noticing. 'I need to do the big reveal!'

'So, reveal away,' I told him, 'then I can leave you in peace to have your own private fashion show.'

Again, the sense of a dark place just at the edge of my mind's eye kept trying to creep back into view. Just where and when did all these 'indecent images' get made? Again, I pushed it down and turned my attention to a pair of pristine trainers that Sammy had now released from the confines of their extensive packaging and out into the wild. I sighed. 'Hmm … very nice. Very *white*. But how many pairs of trainers does one boy need?' I couldn't help but comment, since there were about six pairs already lined up under his chest of drawers.

'But these are wibblesnaps!' he rebuked me. (I'm sure he didn't say 'wibblesnaps' but he might as well have because whatever he did say was similarly incomprehensible. Which meant it was probably trending on TikTok and something only my teenage grandsons would know about.)

Next came another pair of jeans that looked as though they'd been attacked by a rogue pair of scissors, a couple of designer T-shirts (which, bar the logos, looked pretty much like any other T-shirts) and a messenger-style handbag. He must have noticed my puzzled expression at this last item.

'Oh, come on, Casey! Surely you've seen a man bag before?'

Seen one? I'd never even heard of such a thing, not in the real world. But Sammy was quick to educate me. Apparently, anybody who was anybody these days sported one.

'And it's not a gay thing either,' he clarified. 'Not that it would matter if it was. But I promise you, all the trendy male celebs have them. Just Google it and you'll see.'

'It never crossed my mind,' I lied as I stood up and made to leave the bedroom. 'I'll leave you to it, love. I really need to catch up on some laundry and prep the veg – I'm going to do a roast chicken dinner. But come down if you get hungry before tea time, okay?'

'Oh, I'll be fine,' he said. 'We had the most *amazing* dhosas while we were out.'

Which left me equally none the wiser.

Though I'd already decided not to say anything about Jen's visit till later on, it didn't stop me thinking about it, obviously. Principally, I wondered how long this – whatever 'this' was – had been going on for. Most of the children who came to us had pretty big skeletons in their childhood cupboards and many had been victims of some quite sickening adult behaviour before coming into care. But Sammy had only been in the system since he was ten, which threw up an unpalatable scenario. If, as seemed to be the feeling (and today's shopping bonanza only added to the likelihood) something untoward was *still* going on, then that meant the 'system' hadn't protected him at all. Yes, Sammy being in care might have added an extra layer of complication to whatever was happening, but that it was happening under social services' collective noses was a grim thing to think about. There was also the question of how long had it been going on? Had it started at the time of Sammy's grandmother's death? Or, perhaps even more unpalatably, even before that? It was a distressing thing to have to contemplate.

But contemplate it we all must. The boy we'd so far known for a matter of days was suddenly so much more than just a teenager who'd been moved around the system through no fault of his own, tragic though that was. Presumably we would get more detail, but it was already highly likely that Sammy, for all that he *seemed* reasonably stable and sorted, would be carrying some huge psychological problems – not to mention still being embroiled with what appeared, being generous, to be a highly dodgy character – and someone he seemed to see as a cross between a sugar daddy and a father figure.

And now it was my job to wade in and try to help, to try to re-route this troubled life, and however noble the aim and positive the eventual outcome, there was no getting away from it: a big applecart was about to be upset. And that was going to start toppling as soon as Jen did her bit the following day. About which, I knew, I must now tell Sammy. Over dinner. Which so often seems the right time to do things of that nature, second only to being out with a child in the car, where lack of eye contact plus restraining seatbelts makes for the number-one spot.

I'd already told Mike by now and he was helping to keep things light. 'She's not a bad cook, is she?' he joked with Sammy as we all sat down to eat.

Sammy laughed. 'She's not,' he agreed. 'Michelin star quality, this is.'

'Oh, hark at you, Mr "only the best"!' I said. 'Just eat your dinners and less of the sarcasm, please.' And since they were still guffawing, I decided that now was as good a time as any. I hoped to slip it in on the down-low, like a side order of sprouts.

'Oh, before I forget, Sammy,' I said, picking up my cutlery, 'Jen needs to come out and see you tomorrow. You weren't here today, of course, which is fine, but she needs to see you in placement within the first fourteen days, so she has to come back.'

This was actually true and I was banking on the fact that Sammy would already know it.

'Oh my God,' he said, dramatically – or at least faux-dramatically. I was beginning to learn that anything social services-related was responded to similarly melo-dramatically – as if social services were his tedious cross to bear rather than his legal guardians. '*Why?* Why can't they just take a kid to a home, drop them there and then just leave them alone?'

'Well …' I began.

But he was warming to his theme, the knife and fork he'd picked up now held in his hands like batons. 'I don't get why they have to come bother me all the time. Why do they need to do that? No, wait,' he said, pausing for effect. 'I know why. It's to remind us poor unfortunates that no matter where we go, we're different. *That's* what they want us to remember.'

I wasn't sure if this was the product of independent thought or if someone had fed the idea to him, but I suspected the former. He was bright, he'd had lots of time to think. And I was genuinely taken aback. I'd never imagined that some children might feel that way about the people who worked so hard to try and create a safer childhood for them. Yes, lots of kids found social services to be intrusive, but I'd always assumed it was just that; that they were simply taking up their time and they didn't like it.

'I think it's more than that, Sammy,' I said, keen to speak up for my colleagues. 'In fact, I know it is. They stay in your life so you have a kind of constant, and because no matter what other changes go on around you, it's so you at least have *them* to turn to. And that doesn't change.'

Sammy laughed out loud at this. 'Ha!' he scoffed, stabbing his fork into a potato. 'Try telling that to kids who've had about ten social workers come and go. See if they think it's a constant.'

There was no arguing with that because, unfortunately, that was also true for some unlucky children. Not a majority, no, but there was still no getting away from the fact that they represented a significant minority. Through no fault of their own, these children had had the misfortune to be matched with social workers who were set on retiring, or moving up the ladder, or who were simply worn out by the stresses of the job and the unrelenting nature of the workload. And, in the latter case, particularly post the COVID-19 pandemic, the numbers were increasing. Yes, Sammy was obviously plucking the number ten out of thin air – it was a pretty unlikely number – but I did see his point.

And I said so. 'But regardless of that,' I added firmly, 'they *are* here to fight your corner, and they *do* have your back, and with that in mind, Jen is coming to see you tomorrow. I'm sure it will only be a quick visit though,' I continued, as he did one of his heavy sighs, 'so, really, Sammy, I wouldn't stress too much.'

Which felt a bit disingenuous, given what I knew she was going to say to him, but there was no point in giving him any reason to fret about it overnight. Indeed, it would probably be the wrong thing to do so. But thankfully, Mike knew we'd reached the moment for him to change the subject and started talking excitedly about the upcoming new season of some TV sci-fi detective series it turned out they both were mildly obsessed with.

A Family Friend

I ate my dinner as they chatted, glad that my small mission had been achieved, but already agonising about the real stress Sammy was soon going be under when his social worker relayed to him what we all knew. Not to mention the probable consequences, I thought grimly, remembering the pile of purchases upstairs.

Truth be known, though, the abrupt end of Sammy's income stream was only a small part of it. If what we'd learned *was* true – and every instinct in my body told me it was – this was just the tip of a particularly ugly iceberg.

Chapter 6

Not having got to know Sammy that well yet, I wasn't sure how he'd react to Jen's news. It didn't need a genius, however, to take a guess at 'badly'. After all, whatever else he was to the boy, 'Uncle' Kenny was clearly Sammy's long-standing personal cash point – his gifts of money providing a lifestyle most thirteen-year-olds could only dream of.

And so it proved. Since most of the downstairs in our house was open-plan, the only private space I could offer Jen and Sammy for their little chat was our 'snug' – a small room at the front of the house, full of precious knick-knacks (precious to me, that is) and dozens of family photos that Mike and I kept mostly for ourselves. There was also a log burner, a big telly and – a recent addition – the hideous 'posh' glass and gold-plated coffee table I'd reluctantly 'inherited' from Mum and Dad, for 'safe keeping', so foster children and grandchildren were only allowed in with permission.

They'd been in there no more than fifteen minutes when I heard the door open and then slam, followed by the sound of footsteps thundering up the stairs. Jen appeared just as I'd run into the hall.

'Sammy!' she was calling up after him, one hand on the newel post. '*Sammy!*' She then turned to me. 'Well, that went about as well as I expected it would,' she said. 'That is, pretty badly.' She took her hand off the newel post and shook her head slightly. 'I'm not sure I shouldn't just leave him to digest everything – I've a hunch he doesn't want to hear any more from me right now.'

I nodded. 'You're probably right,' I agreed. 'It's only natural to shoot the messenger, isn't it? And he'll probably need some time to process what you've told him anyway. On which note, how much *did* you tell him? Just so I know where we stand.'

'Nothing about the Hawthorne boy's disclosures, obviously. I don't want there to be any repercussions for him. Just that it's come to light – I told him it was as a consequence of doing the normal review of his files undertaken whenever a child moves to a new foster home – that his uncle has a criminal record, which means there is to be no contact between the two of them, and with immediate effect. Which had the immediate effect of whipping him up into a major rage. Again, though, that's hardly surprising, is it?'

'Did you tell him what for?'

'In a manner of speaking,' Jen said. 'Not referring directly to him, of course, but just that the situation relates to allegations regarding child abuse in the past. Obviously don't try to lead any conversations, but do record anything Sammy says that might indicate he knew anything or was part of anything. You know the drill. Anyway, sorry to leave you to handle all this. I don't think I'm going to be much use to you right now, being the devil incarnate ...'

I was tempted to follow my own advice and leave Sammy to collect his thoughts for a bit, while I remained downstairs and started thinking about tea. But I couldn't settle to it; I was worried about him being on his own up there, wondering about the emotions that must be swirling around in his brain. However appalled we might have been by what we'd discovered about this man, the picture was almost certainly very different for Sammy. I knew from experience with other foster children that being cut off from 'Uncle' Kenny wouldn't just have a financial impact for him, this was someone he saw as family – comprised his *only* family now, in fact, since his mother was completely out of the picture. As so often happened with children who'd been groomed by adults who were very close to them, Sammy's emotions would be both complex and deeply perturbing – though on some level he would probably understand the heinous nature of Kenny's activities, this was someone he trusted, and might even love. And if what we knew of the family was true, someone who'd been around for Sammy's whole life.

So, I trotted up the stairs and knocked lightly on his bedroom door. 'Hey, sweetie,' I called, once it was clear that no response would be forthcoming. 'Is it okay if I come in?'

I already had my hand on the handle, and was depressing it, and I imagine he must have seen that because now the answer was immediate: 'Piss off! Okay? Just piss *off*!'

'Sammy, love,' I tried again, 'I just want to check if you're okay. I know this will all have been a big shock for you, and –'

'I *told* you! Piss off! I'm allowed my privacy. Okay? So just leave me alone! And tell Jen she can piss off as well!'

'She's already gone, Sammy,' I reassured him. 'And I understand how you must be feeling. This must all have been a lot to take in and you must have –'

The door flew open then, yanking my hand, still clasping the handle, along with it. I stepped back slightly as Sammy, taut with emotion, now filled the doorway. His cheeks were raspberry pink, his jaw clenched and for a moment I thought he was going to hit me. But the impression disappeared almost as soon as it had come. It was distress rather than rage that I could see on his face. His hands were shaking and his eyes shone with unshed tears.

'Oh, love,' I said, wanting only to soothe him, to hug him. I held back, though. Much as offering physical comfort felt as natural to me as breathing, I didn't want to further invade his personal space so I settled for 'Do you want to sit down and talk about it?'

And I was obviously right not to touch him, because hearing my words made him stiffen even more. 'Don't "oh, love" me!' he barked. 'And no, I *don't* want to talk about it. And it's none of your business *anyway*!'

I could, of course, have gently pointed out that it was, in fact, my business – that *he* was my business, and that the business of caring for him and keeping him safe – well, as far as I could do that – was my job. A job I'd taken on willingly. I wanted to impress upon him that I wanted to help. But these were all things he definitely didn't want to hear right now, so I said none of them, hoping I could somehow convey them to him telepathically.

'I understand, love,' I said instead. 'I can see how much you're hurting. Look, I'll leave you in peace for a bit, shall I? But would you like me to bring you up a coffee? Or a snack? Tea's not going to be ready for an hour or so.'

'No,' he said. '*No*. Just …' I could see him trying hard not to cry. 'Just *leave me alone*. I have nothing to say.'

It seemed an odd thing to say – sounding a little like he was in a police interview room or something, rather than just chatting to me – but that was nothing compared to the oddness of what he said and did next.

Having done as he'd instructed, I was already halfway down the stairs when he spoke again.

'I know what you've been told,' he said, his strange tone causing me to whirl around halfway up the staircase. (I had assumed he'd have retreated back into his room.) 'I know what you people think about me. But if you think I have sex with him, you are *wrong*!'

He took two steps forward so was now standing at the top of the stairs. And then, while I was still digesting this unexpected statement, he laughed – a shrill sound, a high-pitched piece of theatre. He raised both arms as well and threw his head back as he guffawed. 'Look at your face!' he said, flapping his hands around in an 'ooh er!' kind of gesture. '*Yes*, headline news! I've had sex! You think I've never done it? Well, I have. I've had sex with lots of people. Girls *and* boys, for your information!'

It was all so bizarre I could almost feel my jaw dropping. Not only at what he was saying – that was confusing in itself – but the way he was saying it. What was this poor child *actually* trying to communicate to me? And how should I respond? I had no idea if it was true or not – was this thirteen-year-old boasting, or was this an attempt to try and shock me? – but what could I read into him saying something like that? *Was* it just to shock me?

Keen to seize the moment, I opted to make it clear that I wasn't shocked.

'Okay, love,' I said, 'I hear you. But you know, I will have to log this, because it's obviously illegal for anyone to be having sex with a thirteen-year-old, and –'

'Nearly *fourteen*, *actually*,' he shot back, still with this strange theatricality to his tone. 'And there's no point in you doing that, because I would *never* name and shame. Because unlike some, *I'm* not that kind of person.'

So, he was intimating that others were. If so, who? In any event, we seemed to have moved right away from Uncle Kenny. But why? What exactly was going on here?

I had no idea, but that was about to become something of a side issue. Because as I stood there, looking up at him from my position halfway down the stairs, I became aware that he had other matters on his mind. And as I followed his gaze downwards, it became obvious what they were. As I stared in astonishment, a dark stain began to bloom across and down his jeans; he was just standing there, on the landing, and urinating.

'Sammy!' I called out. 'What on earth are you *doing*?'

'What does it look like?' he said, his tone now conversational. 'I've just pissed myself, haven't I? It sometimes happens when I'm stressed and someone is getting on my nerves. Can I be dismissed now?' he finished. 'I need to get changed.'

He then flounced back into his room and shut the door firmly, leaving a puddle on the landing carpet and an acrid smell in his wake.

It was one of the most bizarre things I had ever witnessed in fostering.

Chapter 7

Mike was as baffled as I was. Not just about Sammy urinating in front of me, which had us both scratching our heads, but about the whole 'I've had sex!' thing he'd yelled at me as well. What had all that been about?

'And, more to the point, he's only bloody thirteen years old!' Mike said, shaking his head in disbelief.

It was ten in the evening now, and a very strange evening it had been too. Sammy had remained in his room while I sponged and then scrubbed the landing carpet. And he was almost mocking me, taunting me, it seemed; I could hear him singing along to Taylor Swift as I rubbed cleaning foam into the still-sodden pile. I'd left him to it, though. If he'd hoped to wind me up, he was going to be disappointed. There was no point having another confrontation till I'd got my head around the weirdness of what had happened. And once Mike was home, Sammy trotted straight down for his

65

tea as if nothing *had* happened – had he been watching out for his arrival? And did he really think he could simply shrug off what he had done? Because it was the same when we had our tea and while he helped Mike clear the table. He was chatting away about school stuff, seemingly completely relaxed and happy. Which perhaps he was; was the peeing a bit like self-harming? Did it give him some kind of emotional release? I made a mental note to look further into it.

It was only now, with Sammy in bed, and as we finally got to sit down together, that I'd been able to fill Mike in properly.

'Did he say who he'd had sex with?' he asked now, as we pottered in the kitchen.

I shook my head. 'Nope. Just that he'd done it plenty of times and in a way that suggested I was some kind of old prude for finding that surprising. You know, I'm really beginning to seriously worry about the influence that so-called Uncle Kenny has had on him. But the peeing too – what the hell *was* all that about?'

The question was, of course, rhetorical. I knew only Sammy could answer that with any certainty. Or perhaps he couldn't either. I sighed and pressed the kettle on to make a coffee.

'You want one too?' I asked. 'I know you think caffeine is a bad idea at this time of night, but honestly, love, I'm too wired to sleep right now anyway. I'm going to need to slump in front of something soporific on the TV before going up.'

'Go on then,' he said, reaching for the mugs. 'I'll break my golden rule and join you. I'm not sure I'm going to nod off any time soon either, to be honest. Tell you what, though: I don't think there's much point in cogitating over this, it needs professionals. Suspect your best bet is to call Christine first thing and see if she can press for some psychological support for him.'

So that's what we did. No more trying to work out the many facets of Sammy. Instead, we watched an old episode of the eighties sit-com *Only Fools and Horses* and laughed at the antics of the Trotter family instead.

'Remember, Christine, first thing,' Mike said as we finally got into bed. Then added, in a truly terrible cockney accent, 'You know it makes sense, Rodney!'

Which made me laugh, but the irony wasn't lost on me that making sense out of Sammy was a job for more qualified folks than me.

When Sammy came down for breakfast the next morning and dug immediately into a bowl of cereal, I watched him particularly closely and tried to assess his mood.

'You want any toast and chocolate spread, lovey?' I asked brightly, going with the 'nothing to see here' narrative he was clearly still intent on adopting. 'I got that brand you said you liked.'

Sammy looked up and smiled at me. In his crisp school shirt and trousers, and with his hair neatly brushed, he looked the picture of childish innocence.

'I'm good with just the cereal today, thanks, Casey,' he said. 'We have a cookery lesson this morning – we're learning how to make scones – so I'm going to be stuffing my face again pretty soon.' He then swept an arm down his front. 'And you know me – got to keep my gorgeous on and the pounds off!'

So odd, unreadable Sammy had been replaced with the rainbows and puppies Sammy that we'd first been introduced to. I duly laughed at his joke and turned around to make my own toast. No way was I going to bring up any of yesterday's unsavoury moments when he was being so upbeat. I would definitely save any questions for Christine. And an hour after the transport had picked him up, I was doing just that.

'Wow!' Christine said after I'd filled her in on recent events. 'That is bizarre indeed. And I presume brought about by being cornered, as it were, by his social worker. Is that how you see it?'

'I don't know,' I said, 'but it certainly seems that way, doesn't it? Even so, it's a bit of an extreme reaction. But it's the *way* he did it. He was so calm, so controlled. It really felt like a performance. Like he was doing it specifically to try and shock me. I'm not sure it's the first time he's done it, you know? And yesterday evening, and today, he has seemed completely back to normal. He went off to school like he didn't have a care in the world. Which, again,' I added, 'is rather worrying in itself, considering that Jen had just told him that his main source of income, and the only constant in his life, were both now being taken away from him. What do you think are the chances of getting an urgent meeting with CAMHS?'

'I have a better idea,' Christine said. 'We could get PIPA involved. They tend to act a lot faster than CAMHS and, after all, we've bought the service in so we may as well use it.'

In the last year or so, and often as a preferred alternative to the Child and Adolescent Mental Health Services, or before referring to them, social services had begun using a service called PIPA – short for Psychologically Informed Partnership Approach – where they would 'buy in' a team of clinical and forensic psychologists and advanced practitioners to help a wide range of vulnerable children with varying degrees of trauma and mental health issues.

I hadn't used the service myself yet, but had already heard good things about it on a couple of my fostering WhatsApp groups. Unlike CAMHS, who would act in the here and now, brought in during an immediate crisis, or instead, place a child on quite a long waiting list – often up to two years in length – the way PIPA worked was that, before meeting a child, a psychologist would first be fully briefed on their full history, including any current issues they were dealing with. They could therefore begin building a profile and would then add to it further by having an initial Teams meeting with whoever was the principal carer and sometimes with the child's social worker too.

'Oh yes,' I answered, 'I had forgotten about PIPA. It sounds ideal. Do you think you could arrange that for us, please?'

'Of course,' Christine said. Which was music to my ears and definitely not the sort of thing I was used to hearing. But perhaps that was because PIPA being a relatively new service a lot of people forget they're even there and if they do remember they tend to stick with what they know and don't mind waiting. In addition, it's often a school that will make a referral for a child and they don't have access to the PIPA service.

One thing I did know about our local authority was that they'd bought in quite a large PIPA team compared to some (wisely, in my opinion, given the post-pandemic and still-growing child and teenage mental health crisis) and also believed in using resources that they had paid a lot of money for! All good news for me, of course, but especially in the case of Sammy.

'Oh, and I'll also ask the team who they think it's best to invite to join the initial meeting,' Christine added. 'Could be me, could be Jen. Let's see what they say. Having said that,' she added, 'they might review his file and decided a one-on-one approach – first, you, then Sammy – might be the better way to go. Especially given that Jen's unfortunately *persona non grata* with Sammy right now. Leave it with me, I'll report back as soon as I can. And let me know, of course, if there are any other incidents.'

Which, for the next few days, at least, there weren't. Not at home and, perhaps even more importantly, not at school. Thankfully, the particular traits that were worrying me right now didn't appear to be a problem at school. My end of week 'catch-up call' with Mr Grainger, the teacher who ran the behaviour unit, was all very positive, with him reporting that Sammy had had a lovely week and there had been no concerning issues. 'Well, bar him being found in an area that's out of bounds to pupils from the unit,' he finished. 'But, to be honest with you, that's not an uncommon occurrence. You put any rule in place and there will always be a few who see it as an open invitation to break it, eh?'

I agreed, but there was apparently no harm done.

'And the lad has certainly got his head down since then,' Mr Grainger added. 'Indeed, he's put some very good work in this week. I don't know if he mentioned it, but he's been taking the lead in pulling together a big end-of-term display for a whole school re-wilding project. You might not know, but he's a very talented young artist. So, do not worry. We're looking forward to seeing him again after half term.'

Which was of course very good to hear. You're so often on a knife edge when caring for foster kids with challenging behaviours as keeping them in school, which for the vast majority is exactly where they should be, can be a whole other challenge in itself.

But half term. A reminder that there was another challenge looming. Keeping Sammy occupied, finding ways to coax him out of his bedroom and, equally, away from his phone. For all the positives in my conversation with Mr Grainger, and Sammy's relentlessly upbeat demeanour, it was still a fact that he'd been officially cut off from 'Uncle' Kenny and I'd have to be pretty naive to think that wasn't looming large in Sammy's mind, or that the relationship might not even still be continuing. And how could I even stop that if it was?

It was on the first weekend of half term that a solution presented itself, by way of the stash of art stuff I was storing for my father – and a bit of a head scratch that I hadn't thought of it before.

I was on a rummage in the shed, looking for the clothes airer I'd mislaid, while Sammy was playing keepy uppy with one of Mike's footballs – so perhaps he did 'do' sport after all. And I say 'rummaging' – I was struggling to even get in there, on account of the mass of boxes and bags we were storing for Mum and Dad, which, all these weeks later, were still piled high in a muddle in the middle of the shed floor.

'Sammy, love,' I called to him. 'Could you give me a hand? I need to shift all these boxes and bin bags and make some space, and it's going to take some bigger, stronger muscles than I've been blessed with.'

Needing no further encouragement, he ambled over, flexing his muscles. 'Sure,' he said. 'What needs to go where?'

Having established that it made the most sense to restack all the boxes against the wall at the back, we were soon busy reclaiming order from chaos so we could at least see the wood for the trees. In a flash of efficiency, I'd scrawled details of the contents on most of the boxes so we could quickly establish which of those should go where, with the heavy ones – books, mostly, and china – at the bottom, and clothes and bed linen and 'random drawer contents' (lots of those) going on top. Which still left a load of bags to wade through, and I still hadn't found my clothes airer, but Sammy had found something else instead.

'Ooh, look at this lot!' he cooed, having opened a large, unlabelled suitcase.

I glanced across to see what he was looking at. 'Oh, that's my dad's art stuff,' I told him as he pulled something out, which revealed itself to be a set of acrylic paints.

He turned it over in his hands. 'But it hasn't even been opened! Nor have these,' he said, pulling out another item – this time a three-pack of canvasses.

I went across to Sammy and, looking at the contents of the case, felt a sudden pang of overwhelming sadness. Though Dad had 'dabbled' in his painting hobby for a good few years post-retirement, at some point the passion had clearly ebbed away. I hadn't noticed when I was packing all my parents' belongings, but now I could see that most of the things in the suitcase – palette knives, various fluids, packs of brushes, yet more sets of paints – had never been opened, let alone used. I even recognised a set of oil pastels as having been one I'd bought for him myself – for his birthday, if I remembered right, five or six years ago. It felt so sad that now his painting days were so surely over. But I quickly realised that there was a silver lining here, too: 'Would you like to use them?' I asked Sammy now.

'*Would* I?' he gaped at me. 'You 'avin a larf? Seriously, I would *love* to. I love using acrylics. And I'd really, really love to try oil painting!'

'Then be my guest,' I told him. 'Use what you want.' I then had a thought, remembering back to January, and Riley and I transferring everything from car to shed. 'I'm pretty sure there's also an easel somewhere,' I said. 'You can use that too, if you can find it. But you'll have to look for it, as it's probably buried at the back somewhere. Where I can't risk going … Due to spiders,' I added, in response to his enquiring look. I then threw my hands up, Sammy-style, and pulled a face. 'Because, as everyone knows, I *do* not *do* spiders.'

Sammy laughed, and carefully picked his way to the back of the enormous shed. 'You big scaredy-cat, Casey,' he said as he searched for the easel. 'Spiders aren't scary. Oh my gosh, this is *great*! Thank you, so, so, *so* much.'

'One condition,' I said, already half-regretting what I was about to say. 'No painting in your bedroom, okay? We'll get you set up somewhere in the big room downstairs, so I don't have to worry about getting paint on my carpets.' *Or give you another reason to stay holed up in your bedroom this week*, I thought, but obviously didn't say. And I knew just the place. If I moved the bookcase we currently had in the far corner, I could create a little nook, with plenty of natural light, where he could express himself artistically to his heart's content. I explained where I meant.

'Oh, it'll be like having my own little studio!' Sammy said, clapping his hands together in excitement. 'Oh, thank you so much, Casey, *really*. This week is going to be sick!'

I felt a little sick myself, if I'm honest, though not in the way Sammy meant. I was already imagining the messy chaos that would surely follow but at least I'd found a key to getting him out of his room and, crucially, keeping him productively busy. Which I told myself was a small price to pay, even if one question couldn't help but bubble up. With all that money he'd had in his pockets for so long, how come he'd never spent any of it on art materials himself? I popped the thought into a mental holding bay to chew over later. 'And see if you can find that flippin' airer while you're at it – I bet it's buried under all this stuff somewhere.'

With both airer and easel eventually uncovered, I prided myself on having made a modicum of progress. Perhaps half term wouldn't be so challenging after all. But my confidence, it turned out, was for the birds. Yes, over the next couple of days, Sammy did get himself set up to do his painting and spent a bit of time, here and there, creating artworks, but for the most part he carried on as what I realised was his version of normal, spending the greater part of his time holed up in his bedroom or, if not, the bathroom. He'd often languish for an hour in the bath – especially in the morning – and the second half of the term couldn't come quickly enough.

I particularly worried about him being lonely. When any foster child moved in with us it was always sad that they had had to leave not only their family behind, but also, in most cases, their friends. It's a big problem and a difficult one to solve. These are often friends with whom the child has shared their entire childhood and because these friends always tend to live close to the child's family home, it means there is no chance of them simply hopping on a bus to visit them. In some cases, phone and social media contact is kept up – one benefit of the digital age, at least – but sadly, in most cases it isn't.

It's almost as if, for their own emotional protection, a child decides it's easier to cut all ties: new home, new school, new friends. In Sammy's case, however, he was still going to the same school he'd been to in his last placement so I'd blithely assumed, even if he didn't appear to have a best friend, that he'd at least have a friendship group. But it seemed he really didn't. When I'd asked him earlier if he'd like to ask one of his friends to come over and hang out with him during the holidays, or at weekends – even offering to pick them up and take them home again – he'd replied, 'Oh, I'm a solitary soul, Casey. I don't really *do* friends. My classmates are a bunch of decent kids, I suppose, but they're not like me – we don't have anything in common besides school.'

And that had been that. Another worry to add to my growing list.

Neither, despite my best efforts, could I interest Sammy in coming out with me, including inducements of stops at coffee shops or fancy cafés. I suppose I should have been grateful that he wasn't one of those boys who wanted to be out on the streets all day, but it made life difficult, and the days long, and worried me as well. I did feel that I could leave him while I nipped out to the shops, or round to Riley's or Lauren's for half an hour, and, to be fair, when I returned he was always exactly where I'd left him. But still, if he didn't want to go out with his peers, what I really wanted was for him to at least join in family life and I worried that the reason he wouldn't was because he was still in contact with his 'uncle'.

And it soon came to light that the urinating incident I'd witnessed was just a part of a new and deeper issue.

It was the Wednesday morning and I'd embarked on my usual weekly bedding changeover. Having done our bed and gathered up a fresh set of bedding for Sammy, I knocked on his bedroom door and opened it, as I usually did.

He was on the bed, as per usual, knees up, scrolling on his phone. 'Can you strip your bed for me, love, and let me have your dirty stuff?' I told him, gesturing to the small bundle I was holding. 'I'm going to get a wash on, I've brought you a clean set.'

I duly placed it down on his chest of drawers.

'You mean all of them?' he asked, dragging his eyes away from the screen only reluctantly. 'Though my bedding's fine – I already changed it this morning.'

My first reaction was to smile. How lovely that a boy of his age had gone to the trouble of changing his own bedding. But then I stopped as I realised he'd treated my question as having been in two parts.

'What do you mean, "all of them"?' I asked. 'I just need your sheet, duvet cover and pillow case.'

Sammy threw his phone down on the bed, unfolded himself and went to his wardrobe, then he bent down and scooped up a large pile of laundry. 'There's four sheets here,' he said, holding the bundle out to me. 'I peed the bed a few times, sorry. But I remembered where you kept the clean sheets so I've just been changing them myself. Save you a job, I thought,' he added, his expression bland.

I stared at the laundry he was still holding out for me to take, then at Sammy himself. *Thank heavens*, I thought, *for waterproof mattress protectors*. Then my eyes – I don't know why – were drawn back to the bottom of his wardrobe.

'Sammy,' I said, with a sense of mounting dismay, 'what's in those bottles?' I could see at least four of them, big litre bottles which had previously held sparkling water. And now didn't. Well, I supposed, increasingly horrified, technically they did. But not anymore. Something that was definitely not sparkling, and even at this distance, and in the gloom in there, definitely yellow.

Sammy followed my gaze. 'I'm afraid that's pee too,' he said, inexplicably actually *smiling* at me now. 'I keep meaning to pour them away down the toilet, but forgetting to get round to it.'

I was dumbstruck for a few moments, mostly by his breezy conversational tone. It was as if he was expecting to be mildly chastised for amassing tea plates or dirty coffee mugs. Wetting the bed was one thing, but to actively sit there and relieve himself into plastic bottles, it almost beggared belief. '*Why*, Sammy?' I asked. '*Why* have you been doing this? You are literally *steps* away from the bathroom. Why would you pee in bottles like that?'

Sammy shrugged. 'I don't know why,' he said. 'I guess I'm just lazy. Look, I'm sorry, Casey, I know I shouldn't do it in bottles, but …' He tailed off and shrugged a second time.

'And wetting the bed?' I asked. Because as far as I could ascertain, that was new too. 'Have you always done that?'

He shook his head. 'No,' he said, chattily, 'that one's new.'

I could feel my mouth falling open. 'Then I think we need to get you to a doctor,' I said as I reached to get the pile of sheets from him, which were ominously damp and also hummed. 'Because there's obviously an underlying problem if this is a new thing, and as for the bottles, you need to take them to the bathroom and flush them away – now, please – and then put them in the recycling bin outside. And don't forget to wash your hands thoroughly, too,' I added, imagining the kind of bacterial cultures that would have been merrily proliferating in those bottles. 'Honestly, Sammy, I really just don't get it.'

Sammy laughed then, with that same slightly manic look he'd had when he urinated in front of me, and for a moment I worried he was about to do it again. But instead, he just shook his head. 'I don't need a doctor,' he said, as he bent down to pick up the nearest two bottles. 'I told you, I'm just lazy. Nothing medical about it. It's just a normal teenage thing,' he finished, shrugging for a third time. 'That's all it is.'

But it's not normal, I thought as I watched him grab the remaining bottles and cradle two underneath each arm, before heading off to the bathroom to pour contents of them all down the toilet.

Normal? By any yardstick, this was miles away, *worlds* away, from normal.

Chapter 8

Half term had ended and the start of March brought some pleasingly warm temperatures. This pleased me no end, because it meant I could start leaving open all the windows as the pungent smell of urine coming from Sammy's bedroom had started to permeate the air in the whole house now.

I was still utterly baffled as to why Sammy might be doing this, why he acted as if it was absolutely no problem when he did, and then seemed to conveniently forget it had ever happened in the first place so my session with the psychologist, which was imminent, couldn't come soon enough. Christine phoned me on the Tuesday to tell me she'd sorted it all out and would email a link on the Wednesday morning after Sammy had gone to school so that I could simply click on it at the allotted time and join the meeting.

'It'll be just you, me and the psychologist,' she said. 'Her name is Becky and she's had the full lowdown on

Sammy, so we don't have to waste any of the hour going over his background, including the incidents you emailed me since the last time we spoke.'

Which hadn't exactly been incidents, more discoveries. It was clear that our conversation hadn't changed anything. Sammy continued to wet the bed and to fill bottles with urine on a daily basis and secrete them in his wardrobe. Though 'secrete' was the wrong word – there was no attempt at secrecy whatsoever. And when challenged, he would just shrug and tell me he couldn't help it. So, did I insist he see a doctor? Start bringing in sanctions? It was only the knowledge that this meeting was imminent, and my concern that I might make things worse, that had stopped me.

'That's good,' I said, 'and what's going to happen? Does she ask me questions, or do I just list all our concerns and see what she offers in the way of help?'

'They're all different, the various PIPA workers,' Christine replied, 'but no doubt she will have sketched out a profile by the time she joins us, so hopefully she'll have a clear idea of what you're up against. I suggest though that you make a few notes beforehand, just key points to be addressed and any burning questions you'd like to ask.'

So that's what I'd been working on since our call. In between trying to engage Sammy in everyday life and distract him from the virtual world on his phone, I'd been typing up a document containing the latest incidents, the worries I had and questions about exploitation in general. I had recently completed a new course on child exploitation but that had been quite generic and didn't cover any one particular area in any depth, so I hoped the advice that the psychologist could give me would be more specific.

I was also kind of regretting encouraging and enabling Sammy's new-found interest in art. The drawings and paintings that had been left hanging (by pegs on a makeshift line) in his corner of the living room were a far cry from the ones that were now beginning to be blu-tacked all around his bedroom.

'You like?' Sammy had asked on the Tuesday evening when I took a snack up into his room for him and stared, open-mouthed at his new display. 'I like to call this exhibition "my inner self".'

'Wow,' I said as I took in first one painting and then another, and though I was careful not to show him, not necessarily in a good way. There were demons, a boy who looked as if he was screaming up to the heavens, engulfed in fire, some rather intimate and though stylised, easily identifiable body parts and some paintings of strange, mangled, half animal-half human type beings. 'And these represent *you*?' I asked carefully. 'Or just your thoughts?'

Sammy took the plate of buttered crumpets from me and set them down on his desk while he sat on the stool, head bowed, resting on his fist, looking for all the world like a comical image of *The Thinker* sculpture.

'Is there a difference?' he said finally. 'Because I'm thinking that if these paintings are what I'm thinking about at the time I do them, then they must actually be a part of me, don't you think?'

He looked up at me, smiling, and I honestly couldn't work out if he was teasing me, or genuinely trying to explain his gory artwork.

I smiled back. 'I'm not sure, love,' I said, 'and I'm definitely no artist, by any stretch of the imagination, but I've heard that all art is expression of some form and gives us the freedom to explore any subject matter, no matter how dark. But I suppose when you look at other forms of art – say, writing, for example – the fact that Stephen King writes horror stories doesn't make him a serial killer or something, does it? So, I suppose there's a difference, wouldn't you say?'

I had absolutely no idea where that little bit of information had come from, or even if I was remotely right in what I'd said, but it was all I could come up with in answer to Sammy's strange question. Either way, it seemed to satisfy him as he then grabbed his pencil and sketch pad and beamed back at me.

'Thanks, Casey,' he said. 'I'm feeling all inspired now and thanks for the crumpets as well. Fuel for the tortured artist! Anyway, I'll get on.'

And that was my dismissal. I shuddered as I glanced once again at the image of the burning boy and went back downstairs to the living room. This time, rather than just glance at the paintings he'd strung up in there,

84

I really studied them. But no, there was nothing unto-ward about these ones. Self-portraits, what looked like fashion sketches, a bowl of fruit and a scene that was obviously inspired by our back garden. They were good, too. His teacher was definitely right about his artistic talent but this stuff was so different from what was upstairs. *Question the art?* was the next thing I typed up on my list of concerns.

I took myself and my laptop into our snug for the Teams meeting on Wednesday morning. My friends and all my family knew that if they called in to see me and I was tucked away in the snug, then I was either in a virtual meeting or on an important call. They would then make themselves a drink and wait for me, or leave and call back later. I had also taken in a full jug of coffee and a few biscuits, because no meeting was complete without biscuits, even if it was virtual, and I would scoff them all myself.

Some foster carers still raged about the lack of face-to-face meetings these days and hated the online sessions, but I loved them. As long as I put a bit of make-up on and tied up my unruly curls, then I could attend the meeting in my pyjamas and dressing gown if I liked. What was not to love? Today though, I was dressed, albeit in just leggings and a T-shirt, but dressed all the same.

I waved to Christine, who'd appeared in the corner of my laptop screen, and smiled at Becky, the psychologist, as she introduced herself.

'I know you're fully aware of the service PIPA provides,' she started, 'so I'll skip all the formalities and we'll just get on with it. Now, Casey, Christine and I have already had a ten-minute catch-up. That doesn't cut into our hour, obviously, but she's outlined a few things for me, so if you could just quickly run through a bit of a timeline of events since Sammy moved in with you guys, that would be very helpful – just skim over the details, if you would, and we can re-visit each point afterwards.'

I did as she asked, mentioning the flamboyancy, the Kenny concerns, the urinating incident and the revelations about sex, the bed wetting, the constant peeing in bottles and, more recently, the strange artwork he'd made. I read from my notes and noticed that Becky was taking notes herself, the whole time I was speaking.

'Christine?' she asked when I finished, 'anything to add to that?'

Christine glanced at her notes. 'Only about the incident at the Hawthornes' house, with their son, and the background to that. Have you got that on your file?'

Becky nodded and removed her glasses. 'I have – I have a really in-depth report in front of me, as well as my own analysis and a few suggestions for you guys going forward. First of all, Casey, I have also got copies of all of your daily logs and I'd like to say that you're doing everything right, so don't worry – I'm not here to teach a grandmother to suck eggs. I'm aware you have a long and excellent record. It just sometimes helps to get an extra pair of eyes, with a fresh perspective at times, doesn't it?'

'Thanks,' I said, smiling. This woman really knew how to put folk at ease and I instantly liked her. She looked to be in her late forties or early fifties, with a soft, genuine smile. Also, she somehow seemed to radiate intelligence. 'Yes, I'm grateful for any input or help you can offer.'

'Okay then, so here are my thoughts,' Becky said, putting her glasses back on. 'I'm just going to open another screen on my laptop so I can see all the reports and my analysis, etc. Just bear with me a sec.'

I was impressed. I'd never mastered the art of multiple screens – this lady was obviously the real McCoy.

'So, we have to assume that Sammy has been sexually exploited in some form,' she told us. 'And I think it's safe to say that this Kenny fellow may have been part of that. In my opinion, Sammy will not be ready to make any disclosures at this point. He's an intelligent lad and he will know what a disclosure would mean for all concerned. The truth is that in cases like this, we may *never* get to the bottom of it. Sammy might not ever discuss the details, and without a confession from the perpetrator themselves, there is nothing we can do about that, unfortunately.'

I gaped at her. 'What, even if we're sure?' I asked. 'Even if all the signs are there?'

'Nope,' Becky said, 'but if we believe it, which we do, I guess, then what we can do is to act as though it *is* true and support Sammy, like we would any other abused child. That is, we leave the door open for them to talk whenever they are ready, we look at their behaviours, such as the urinating, and we suppose it's because they are reacting to such a shocking trauma and we treat it accordingly.'

She went on to explain that in Sammy's case the bed wetting and the peeing in bottles was probably a form of control. That maybe he felt that parts of his body had been taken from him and rather than face that head-on, the only way he knew to control those certain parts was to not follow convention with them. I sort of understood the thinking behind it and immediately admonished myself internally for sometimes believing Sammy was being disrespectful, or just trying to wind me up.

'A child who's been abused may not ever tell another adult about it,' Becky said, 'but they will always tell you, *without* telling you, if you know what I mean. The artwork, for example. Sammy showed you that he can draw and paint. You knew that because both a teacher and he himself told you. But he also wanted to *show* you, without verbal explanation, the type of painting that he was good at, how he'd like to see the world, i.e. the paintings you describe as being up in your lounge, but he also needed to show you the real world he came from, via the messed-up, crying-for-help artwork he reserved for the privacy of his own room. He won't explain this to you, but he's aware. His little question to you about whether they represent his thoughts or himself show me that he's very aware.'

This all made so much sense. As did Becky's explanation about Sammy's obsession for buying things and his outlandish fashion choices. The almost compulsive buying – mainly clothes, jewellery and expensive colognes – was all about transforming his physical self into what he saw as a carefree, respectable person. An exterior persona of someone who didn't have a care in the world, to disguise his internal pain and lack of self-worth.

This part, of course, was very straightforward to understand. Why did anyone cover themselves in expensive designer logos, after all? To gain approval. To say to the world 'I am a person of high status'. I got that, but I was still a bit unsure about the control thing Becky had mentioned earlier.

'Sorry to press the issue,' I said, 'and I sort of understand about the peeing in bottles and bed wetting now, but how do you reckon I should respond to that when it happens next?'

Becky flicked back a page of the large notebook she had in front of her before answering.

'Right, so here's the thing. Your reaction was one of shock at first, and then possibly a little anger, and, I'm guessing now, mostly irritated about it all, yes?'

I nodded, smiling, but also feeling a little bit guilty. 'That's more or less exactly how it went,' I admitted.

'So, my thoughts are that Sammy now knows that he's exposed a little of his trauma to you and yet your reactions are still suggesting that you don't understand it. From now on, I want you to try to convey to Sammy that you're hearing him, without actually saying it.'

Becky went on to suggest that the next time I was confronted with either bottles of pee or wet sheets, I should look Sammy in the eyes, smile and nod at him, and simply retrieve the sheets without saying anything. As for the bottles, she said I should perhaps just mention them as an afterthought, on my way out of his room, her suggestion being something along the lines of, 'oh, and Sammy, love, if you have any bottles to empty, make sure you sort them out this morning'. She reckoned that my simple acknowledgement of his deeper issues just might be enough to make it stop.

Even though it all made perfect sense now that Becky had explained it to me, it was also revelatory. I left that meeting with a renewed sense of determination regarding Sammy. This poor kid was trying to shed his pain in the way a snake sheds its skin. Yet despite all the advice to not push on the Kenny issue – Becky had made very clear that I should leave that be for now – I still felt that he was the one particular snake that had caused all this trauma and I wouldn't rest until he had been stamped on. The poison might already be too deeply rooted for Sammy to be able to talk about it, but that didn't stop those in power doing their very best to tease it out.

Chapter 9

Over the next couple of weeks, all I could really do was try my very best to keep a watchful eye over Sammy. Now that he was back in school I was pleased to see that he was beginning to go out a little, here and there. But where? Because when I quizzed him, it appeared that it wasn't to meet up with anyone – it was just 'for a bit of fresh air and exercise', as if he'd been given that as a prescription by a GP. Worryingly, however, whenever I suggested that I might accompany him (which was often), he always rejected this idea by pointing out that it was important 'alone time' he needed and that walking by himself got his creative juices flowing and gave him new inspiration for his art.

How could I argue with that, or indeed try to stop him? I simply didn't have the authority to, and Sammy knew that. And it made me a little nervous every time he left the house as I was both anxious he might just decide to run off, or be secretly contacting 'Uncle'

Kenny while he was away from us. Because that too was impossible to control. Sammy had his phone, his internet and bank card downloaded – all things I had no access to and no authority to inspect. I just had to trust that now that he *knew* that he wasn't allowed contact with Kenny, then his 'uncle' would know it too and the pair of them – especially Kenny – might now leave it alone rather than risk police involvement.

I was glad therefore when I got a call from James, Sammy's outreach worker, towards the end of March.

'I thought I'd nip across this afternoon,' he said, 'when Sammy gets home from school and take him out for tea, if that's okay with you?'

'That would be great,' I said, and meant it. 'I'm just doing a salad for Mike and me, and Sammy hates salad apparently, so I was wondering what to make him instead. It turns out you've saved me a job. So yes, thank you. Offer gratefully accepted.'

Although I didn't say it, it also set me at ease because at least the boy wouldn't be going out alone tonight and that was one less thing for me to worry about.

I told Sammy as soon as he got home and was pleased that he seemed happy about it. 'Yes!' he trilled, with a little fist pump. 'I best go get myself ready then, hadn't I? Now, what to wear, what to wear … I don't suppose he said where we'd be eating, did he?' This, all as he was running upstairs, his school backpack still swinging from his shoulder.

I didn't know what had prompted James's unexpected visit, though I suspected, and happily, that Christine might have been involved. I laughed and called after him, 'He didn't, love, no, but I'm sure whatever you choose will be just fine.'

Or not, I thought, picturing his various outfits.

James arrived right on time in his little Mini and I watched as he strode up our drive, clearly stretching out each leg as he walked. Again, I thought, what an odd choice of vehicle it was for such a tall man. I called Sammy downstairs and as I opened the door and glanced to my left, I had to stifle a chuckle at the vison in white that had appeared beside me. Was it a shirt? Was it a blouse? Was it a christening robe? It was anyone's guess, but it was very sheer and the incoming breeze readily made it billow open to reveal an equally white vest top underneath and one of his signature pairs of very pale, artfully ripped jeans.

'Do my sliders look okay with this, Casey?' he asked, as if I was the epitome of a fashion-forward expert, whose opinion might be a game changer for him. James was still taking it all in. Sammy smiled at him too now. 'Or should I put my Docs on, d'you think? Give it more of an edge?'

I looked down at his feet with the designer brand flip-flops – the sort of thing my gran would have slipped her feet into to keep her feet warm on cold lino. 'They look great,' I began, but James interjected.

'Mate, it's March,' he said, 'and we might end up walking for a bit. I'd go for the Docs, if I were you.'

The question of 'edge or not' having been settled, albeit obliquely, Sammy slipped his feet from the offending footwear and ran back up the stairs.

'How's it going?' James asked.

'As well as can be expected,' I answered. 'He still hasn't said anything outright about Kenny, but Christine told me she'd updated you on everything and said you'd been asked to watch out for any red flags and report back, yes?'

He nodded. 'He's normally quite open, but he's never mentioned a word about any of that to me, but yes, if he does, I'll pass it on.'

We heard Sammy running back downstairs just then so our conversation was halted but I was pleased to know that James was fully aware of everything.

'Docs it is,' Sammy said as he joined us. 'I think they look rather dapper actually – I don't know why I didn't go for these first.'

'Right,' I said. 'And I'm sure your toes are going to thank you. Now go on and enjoy your tea.'

'Oh, I will,' Sammy said as he skipped off alongside James to the car. 'And you guys enjoy your rabbit food!'

With an hour to spare until Mike arrived home and a good couple of hours before I expected Sammy back, I decided to phone Riley for a catch-up. It wasn't like rabbit food needed a lot of prep, after all.

'Why don't you nip round for a coffee, Mum?' she said as soon as I told her Sammy had been taken out. 'Our Kieron's over with the little ones while Lauren's taking her mum to the podiatrist so it'll be an opportunity to catch up with them too.'

I obviously didn't need to be asked twice so after sending Mike a quick text to let him know where I'd gone, I was in the car and on my way. It was only five minutes' drive at that time of day and Riley had a coffee waiting for me as I stepped through the door.

'Nana!' The kids called out en masse as they each showered me with hugs and kisses. It didn't matter how old they got, they never tired of the hugging and kissing, and there is absolutely no question that, particularly as a grandparent, a child's uninhibited delight at the sight of you was a better gift than anything anyone could ever buy. Like a vitamin shot for the soul.

As they resettled back into the various things they'd all been doing, it made me feel a pang of sadness for poor Sammy though. How might things have been different for him if his nana hadn't died? I'd never known her and – no surprises – Sammy had never spoken about her at all, but I had fixed her in my mind as a strong, loving presence and a woman who'd have knocked her 'friend' Kenny's lights out if she'd still been alive.

'Just what I needed,' I told my daughter as she handed me a mug of coffee. 'Not this, I mean,' I qualified, nodding out to where the younger ones were back running around the garden. 'But this too, of course.'

'He been giving you a hard time, Mum?' Kieron asked. 'Riley was just telling us all about him. It does all sound a little bit suspicious about that uncle character, doesn't it?'

Keiron put the word 'character' in finger quote marks and I smiled inwardly. My son's nature was such that he found it extremely difficult to think ill of anyone, so this was quite a bold statement for him.

'It does,' I agreed. 'But no, not a hard time at all. It's just a bit stressful, as always, and that goes with the territory, I suppose, but it's harder because he's such a loner. I'm really struggling to get him out of his bedroom and taking part in any kind of ordinary family life.'

'A *little* bit?' Riley scoffed, shaking her head at her younger brother. 'Stay as sweet as you are, babes. But, you know, Mum, holing up in bedrooms is kind of standard behaviour for teenage boys, isn't it?' She nodded towards Keiron and grinned. 'As you already know!' Then jerked out of the way as he went to play-punch her on the arm.

We both knew she was probably right though. When he was a teenager, Keiron's bedroom wasn't just his bedroom. For a time, it was pretty much his entire world. And Riley's boys, Levi and Jackson, my two eldest grandsons, were definitely following suit, what with their ever-present phones and their passion for gaming. But Sammy's solitary nature was on another level and not, was my hunch, because he didn't like company. He was an articulate, sociable boy. And it definitely wasn't gaming that he was up to. He just retreated too much into his virtual world; tipping over into the deeply unhealthy.

A Family Friend

'Why don't you take him bowling with Ry and co at the weekend?' Kieron suggested, ever the problem solver. 'Me and Laur can't go now. You could take Dad as well so he could show Sammy some of his moves an 'ting.' He laughed. As we all usually did. Not that I often accompanied any members of my family to any bowling alleys. I once got my finger stuck in a ball and it nearly took me with it. My being sprawled out on the lane while everyone else stood and guffawed was a memory that still haunted me today.

'That's actually a nice idea,' Riley said. 'It's just going to be us and Levi and Jackson, too, because Marley Mae's on a sleepover with her mate. And you never know, him and the boys might get along really well. Worth a try if he'll agree to it, don't you think? Now, then, can I offer you one – no, five – of Jackson's cheese and basil scones?' she asked 'Cookery today in school. You are *not*, *repeat*, *NOT* allowed to say no.'

I was touched, heading home an hour later with my little Tupperware pot of much-maligned scones. I tried not to ever force any of my foster children on my family – I never wanted them to think they had some sort of duty towards them, especially with their own family lives so busy these days. Though when it happened, which it often did, and a kid grew close to the wider Watson clan, it invariably was a positive for all concerned. So, I happily took Riley up on her suggestion and put it to Sammy as soon as he got home, having agreed with Mike that we'd frame it as having already been booked, thus non-negotiable.

And his immediate willingness to agree to the outing quite surprised me. Till he added, having already told me about his visit to a cool cat café with James, that it would be the perfect place to film some great content.

'Cat café?' Mike wanted to know. 'What's a flippin' cat café when it's at home? The mind boggles! What's wrong with them serving sandwiches and cake?'

Sammy rolled his eyes and laughed. 'It's a café where a bunch of cats live and they, like, hang out with you and let you stroke them. It's good for wellness,' he added. 'I'm not sure it was quite the sort of thing James was into – I think he's a bit allergic – but I saw it on Instagram, and –'

'Ah,' I said, feeling for poor obliging James. He'd been rubbing his eyes when he dropped Sammy home and hurried off to his next appointment. '*Now* the penny's dropping ...'

'I think I'll wear my black jeans and baseball boots,' Sammy said, already moving on to his sartorial choices. 'And a black T-shirt – keep it simple,' he mused. Then he frowned. 'God, though, you have to put on those *hideous* shoes when you get there, don't you?'

'Yes, but everyone does,' Mike pointed out, 'so we'll all look uncool together.'

As withering looks went, Sammy's towards Mike was priceless: 'Speak for yourself!' he admonished.

* * *

Whatever the motivation Sammy might have had for agreeing to have an evening out with us, it went really well and watching him chatting to Levi and Jackson warmed my heart. Yes, it was a little dispiriting how often he got his phone out to take selfies, or asked the boys to take multiple snaps of him posing, but that definitely wasn't something out of the ordinary; even just a cursory glance around confirmed that everyone under a certain age seemed to be doing the same. He even grabbed a couple of shots of me, too, thrusting his phone in front of me and saying, 'Smile, Casey!' Little monkey! I hate having my photo taken at the best of times, especially when I'm not prepared for it and unable to artfully rearrange all my lumps and bumps. Was I going to end up on his 'gram too? Perish the thought!

I hadn't reckoned on quite how much my daughter was studying him, however. 'I know you're probably used to it,' Riley said to me when we were sat in our booth having a rest, 'but God, it's like he has loads of personalities, isn't it? And like he's trying them all out on us. One minute he's kind of just like Levi and Jackson, like a normal teen, the next he's all bloody Louie Spence from *Pineapple Dance Studios* – flouncing about, all "dahling" this and "dahling" that!'

I couldn't help but laugh at the image she'd created. And it was true – Sammy could often be very over-the-top camp. But I took her point. It didn't seem innate. He could definitely switch it on and then switch it off again. And I wondered how conscious these behaviour switches were. It put me in mind of a little girl I'd fostered only recently, who, aged six, would from time to time regress to being a toddler and babble nonsense instead of using real words. As with so many behavioural tics I'd witnessed over the years, I was always told it was probably a way of getting attention, even if the child didn't know they were doing it. Was it like that for Sammy? Was this more of him speaking to me without actually speaking?

I didn't let it spoil my enjoyment of the evening, however, which turned out, we all agreed, to have been a great success and something I hoped we could repeat before too long. In the meantime, the daily reality continued; he was still wetting the bed and still peeing in bottles, and despite my remembering the psychologist's advice and giving it an obvious non-reaction it was still happening several times a week.

'I'll arrange another PIPA session,' Christine said when I told her about it on our call around the middle of the following week. 'But this time, I'll see if Becky will speak with Sammy directly, on his own. It will depend what she thinks,' she went on. 'As I said, it's never a given that they'll work one on one with a child as they prefer the strategies they suggest to be implemented by the child's carers, but it might be the case that she feels she might get more from Sammy herself. We shall see.'

'I'm happy either way,' I told her. 'Just do your best. I'd love to continue because it really is a problem – and not just because I have extra laundry and the knowledge I'll probably have to get rid of that bed. There's clearly something very, very much amiss with the poor boy.'

Christine agreed she'd get on to it and let me know as soon as she did, and in the meantime I just had to accept that for now – my duty was to simply love and care for Sammy and leave any mental health problems to other professionals. Thankfully, other than that, home life and school life seemed to be pretty much smooth sailing. That was until the last day of March, when I got the call from Sammy's school.

I say 'the' call, because with a foster child who has a history of behavioural challenges, you're always half-expecting it. And, appropriately enough, when it came, the meteorological weather had changed too, a howling March wind battering my windows with heavy rain. No chance of doing anything other than cleaning in this weather, I had already decided, and so, braced for some extreme housework, I was still in my dressing gown when the phone went at half eleven.

'I know it's a terrible day,' Mrs Masters said to me after introducing herself as Sammy's head of year, 'but we've just had an extremely concerning report about Sammy and I wondered if you were able to come in.'

Oh no, I thought, *I bet he's wet himself or something*. But that 'extremely concerning' seemed to suggest it must be something more than that. 'What's happened?' I asked, to double-check before I jumped to conclusions. 'Is it something he's done?'

'I'd rather you came up to the school as soon as you can,' she said. 'It's not really something I can discuss on the phone, but the report came from a female friend of Sammy's, Erin – do you know her?'

I automatically searched my mind, but knew there would be slim to no pickings to be found there. Had Sammy ever mentioned the name of *anyone* other than Kenny? 'I'm afraid not,' I said, truthfully. 'In fact, he's never actually mentioned a friend to me at all.'

I tried again to push for an explanation about why whatever it was had been 'concerning', but it was clear Mrs Masters wanted to see me face to face before telling me more, so I promised her I'd be there within the hour. Then I shot upstairs, showered, dressed and gathered my bits together. And as I found my car keys and flung on a thick waterproof jacket, I had the unmistakable feeling of anticipation, not wholly negative, that a can of worms was about to be opened. Because at least it meant that I could peer in and better see what they looked like.

Chapter 10

I stepped outside, hood up, and the wind immediately whisked it off my head again, throwing cold rain onto my face as it did so. Though the temperature had risen a little, it had obviously been begrudgingly, expressing its mood by replacing the crisp spring sunshine with my two least favourite types of weather. Brilliant. I flipped the hood up again and held it tightly under my chin as I climbed into my car. At least, I mused, it matched my current frame of mind: squally showers, storms expected.

I plugged my phone into the car USB port and entered the school postcode I'd been given. It was going to be a thirty-minute drive and to a part of town – well, actually more the outskirts – that I didn't know well.

School behaviour units I did know, however. Before I made the switch to fostering, I'd been a school behaviour unit manager – a job I'd done, and loved doing, for several years. It was doing that job, in fact, that led me to consider the idea of fostering. Spending time in school with looked-after children meant that I got to know several dedicated foster carers and the more I saw the more I thought it might be something I could do too. It had been a good decision. Much as I'd enjoyed my former job, I realised I'd found my passion and had never looked back.

So here I was, on the other side of the equation, as I had by now been lots of times before. And was no stranger, therefore, to the sort of set-up I imagined I'd find: a hotch-potch of kids, drawn from across different age groups, some with behavioural issues – the bullies and sometimes, too, the bullied – and others who, often due to challenging home lives and family set-ups, found it hard to thrive in the social maelstrom of a big, busy high school. There were almost invariably neurodiverse kids in such units as well; kids who struggled both with the way education was delivered, and with relationships with their peer groups, the 'rules' of which sometimes overwhelmed them.

It was something I understood from personal experience. My own son Kieron had been diagnosed as neurodiverse in early childhood, though back then the term they used was Asperger's syndrome, a diagnosis that, having become so controversial, was no longer in use. These days, it would be classed as a mild autism spectrum disorder, or ASD. Kieron, with all his peccadillos and his funny little ways, had been through the same mainstream education as his friends, always accompanied by his Statement of Special Educational

Needs, and trying his best to make sense of the world and fit in.

Kieron had worked his way through it and, as an adult, had found his feet and didn't find life quite as challenging, even if he still had his peccadillos and idiosyncratic little ways. But these days, with much greater knowledge about neurodiversity generally, it was the education system itself that was working hard to adapt and accommodate. To my mind, that equalled positive progress. Till the happy day, though, when a lot more kids could thrive in the mainstream, units such as the one Sammy attended were a much-needed refuge for all kinds of 'misfits', as they would once have been known, providing sanctuary for kids who might otherwise not attend school at all.

Which thought brought another, more dispiriting one, with it. Given what I'd been told over the phone, was Sammy now going to be excluded? Knowing what I knew, and what we were dealing with at home, the words 'extremely concerning' spoke volumes.

The rain and wind didn't let up for the entirety of the journey and by the time I entered the main school, having parked in the far-distant visitors' car park, my showerproof coat was literally streaming with water. Stamping a couple of times and shaking off as much as I could, I headed into the welcome warmth, my senses immediately prickled both by the smell of lunch, which drifted less than tantalisingly in the air, and the rumble of familiar sounds that only a secondary school makes.

Every school these days is security-minded, so it was no surprise to be greeted by one of the school secretaries from behind a glass wall. I told her who I'd come to see and signed the proffered visitor log. Then, having taken off my raincoat and turned it inside out, I went and sat where directed in one of a brace of low upholstered chairs that had seen much better days. Over to my left, across a wide expanse of floor, was a huge display board on which various achievements were proudly noted. Sports awards, teams of children beaming out, clutching medals, posters detailing upcoming events, including a production of *Les Misérables*, all topped off by the usual bracing school slogans. There were also several artworks, big and small, displaying considerable talents – might Sammy get a chance to grace this space one day? I wondered how the current art project for the school hall was going. Was it up yet? And would Sammy still be here to see it, if not?

'Mrs Watson?'

I turned to see a woman approaching. She had that capable look I had come to associate with heads of years in secondary education, having met and worked with several in my time. Her warm smile put me at ease straight away.

I stood up and nodded. 'That's me. Mrs Masters?'

'Indeed I am. Come along, I've managed to find an office we can talk in. Sorry to drag you all the way here like this,' she added, as I followed her down an adjacent corridor. 'We just felt it best that we speak face to face rather than on the phone to see if we can find a sensible way through this.'

She stood back by a half-open door and ushered me through it, into a small room stuffed to bursting with books and piles of paperwork. It wasn't clear what its purpose was other than desk space and a dumping ground, but it had a couple of armchairs, one of which she directed me to.

'So,' she said, taking the other, 'let me run through what we know of the situation, which has been ongoing for a couple of weeks now, it appears.'

Mrs Masters went on to explain what form Sammy's 'extremely concerning' behaviour had taken. And, as I'd half-expected, it involved him urinating. But it had been worse than just that. Not only had he apparently been doing that, and in inappropriate places, he'd been asking his friends to film him doing it as well.

'The set-up here,' Mrs Masters explained, 'is that the children in the unit generally don't much come into contact with the main school. Their building is on the other side of the grounds and though they aren't supposed to mix during the school day, and go in for lunch fifteen minutes earlier than everyone else, it does sometimes happen – children coming back from break and lunch late so they can hang out with their mainstream mates. It's hard to strike a balance, as I'm sure you'll know.'

'How many do you have in your unit?' I asked, not knowing what mix of pupils Sammy spent his school days with.

'It varies, but there are usually fifteen or sixteen in there at any given time. A few are there long-term – such as in Sammy's case. But others are only there for a short while as we monitor the situation, or work out a longer-term plan for them. In this case, however, it's a girl from the main school – my year group, same as Sammy – who alerted us to what's been going on.'

And what had been going on made for depressing listening. Though Sammy had told me more than once that he didn't 'do' friends, it seemed he did when it suited him to. Because according to Mrs Masters, and against the rules in place for children in the unit, he apparently managed to meet up regularly with a little group he'd been in while still in mainstream education. And what had started out, in the girl's words, as just a 'bit of silly stuff to put on TikTok' – filming him peeing up walls and into various receptacles and so on – had taken a much darker turn. The previous week he'd performed – and wanted another boy to film – an entire striptease, going as far as bending over and asking the boy to get close-ups of his bottom.

Mrs Masters was too much of an experienced teacher to look at all shocked by what she was now relating to me – we both knew the sort of horrors that could be found on that particular platform – but her finishing head shake and sigh said it all. Though the boys involved had apparently found it funny – no more out of bounds than, say, mooning out of a car window, not in their book, anyway – the girl felt a line had been crossed and said so. Squaring up to Sammy, she'd asked him why he would want to do something like that – have his naked body plastered all over the internet for all to see – and it was his answer that prompted her to act.

'"Three hundred quid," he had told her, apparently. "Simple! Three hundred quid – just like that!"' Mrs Masters spread her hands, palms up, then smiled wryly. 'I mean, you think you've seen it all, but …'

I shook my head and sighed my agreement. In both our lines of work, we obviously did tend to think that, but perhaps as part of the online revolution, teenagers always seemed to find new ways to make even the been-there-done-that, long-in-the-tooth types like us roll our eyes.

'So, the question is what to do next. I'm assuming you'll have some thoughts on this. Have you had your own concerns about this kind of thing?'

To which the answer could only be yes, so I admitted as much and told Mrs Masters all about the kind of challenges we were facing at home. The urinating ones, obviously, both in front of me and into bottles, and our fears – no, more than that, I said, our growing conviction – that Sammy had been the victim of sexual abuse, and who from, even if at this point in time I had no concrete evidence, so couldn't yet prove it.

'So, the fact that he mentioned doing it to get money is actually slightly heartening,' I said. 'I know that sounds an odd thing to say, but the fact that he's actually said that to another pupil will add a bit of weight – perhaps give us a little more clout. Because if he's sharing images online, I'm pretty sure that's against the law.' I sighed then, thinking of the bigger picture. But that would, of course, mean that the no-contact rule was being flouted.

Yet again, Mrs Masters' expression remained calmly attentive. No one in education is ever less than alert for that particular canker on society, for obvious reasons – they get to see the results of it all the time.

'Or there is no longer any contact and he's going it alone,' she countered. 'Surely that's equally possible? Either way, it's equally dispiriting. And, yes, in answer to your question, it is indeed against the law and we'll leave Sammy in no doubt about that. Oh, dear, it's all so sad, isn't it? He's a bright lad, I'm told …' She shook her head. 'Bright, but so blighted.'

I nodded. 'He's also been doing a lot of painting at home – he's a talented artist, as you know, and I've given him my father's old art stuff to use. But some of the stuff he produces is, to say the least, pretty disturbing to look at. It's him "telling us about the abuse without having to verbally tell us", or so the PIPA counsellor says.'

'Ah, so you've got him some counselling?'

I shook my head. 'Not Sammy himself, not as yet. We've just had initial meetings – her and I, plus my supervising social worker – to try and work out some strategies for how I need to handle things going forward. I imagine the next step will be for Sammy to have some sessions with her too, though it's early days. He's *highly* averse to talking about himself. Fashion, yes, his inner demons not so much.'

'Well, we can make a positive contribution there at least,' Mrs Masters said, her voice now reassuring. 'We've had no ongoing issue here with Sammy,' she continued. 'He's never done anything inappropriate before – not that we've been made aware of, not until this came to light, at least – and, given his age, we think the best next step is simply to call him in and let him know we're aware. We have a "no phones in class" policy, which we're currently reviewing – the children are allowed to use their phones when not in class at the moment, but we're leaning towards a "no mobiles in school at *all*" policy – not before time, in my opinion – and this seems further grist to that particular mill. And going forward, I've spoken to the behaviour unit manager, Mr Grainger, and the head, and we propose that as well as letting Sammy know that uploading such images as have been described to me to the internet would constitute a criminal offence, against Section 1 of the Children Act 1989, we'll set him up with weekly counselling sessions here right away as well – partly to educate him more fully about staying safe online, but also to explore, as far as we can, anyway, why he feels the need to do it. Well, over and above that three hundred pounds he mentioned,' she added wryly. 'Try to go through the many scenarios the term exploitation can refer to, so he understands more clearly how others can manipulate children for their own financial gain. And, even if it does appear to fall on deaf ears, I'm a great believer in keeping on keeping on, as' and here she paused and smiled 'I'm sure you are as well.'

'One hundred per cent,' I agreed. 'It's just all so frustrating. He's obviously still embroiled with this man, even if he's currently lying low, and we're so toothless in terms of getting Sammy out of his clutches. Yes, we can restrict his access to the internet while he's at home, but short of taking away his phone, which we're obviously not allowed to do, it's impossible to stop it – to even police it, to be honest. But he *so* needs to understand that he's being exploited by this man. Needs to work that out for himself, ideally. So, the counselling here will be very helpful. Thank you. So what happens next? I'm assuming you've not spoken to Sammy himself as yet?'

Mrs Masters shook her head. 'No, we wanted to run everything by you first.' She glanced up at the big wall clock. 'I've one more parent meeting to get done first and then I'll be calling Sammy in for a chat and asking Mr Grainger to join us. I intend to let Sammy know exactly what we've been told and that you are also aware now, and I'll try to get him to tell me what he was doing and why. I'll also make it clear that what I've outlined to you will be happening and that he *must* sign up to it, including the meetings with the school counsellor. So,' she said, her hands palms down on the chair arms, signalling she was about to stand up and that the meeting was over, 'a team effort, eh?'

A Family Friend

She stood up. As did I, following suit so I could leave her to continue working her way through her doubtless very busy day.

There was a poster on the corridor wall as I walked beside Mrs Masters back to the reception. It was full of slogans and one immediately jumped out at me: 'Knowledge is power,' it said. I could not agree more. Now we had some of the former, via the evidence of that brave girl who'd felt empowered to stand up to and challenge Sammy, I felt that, of the latter, we had just a smidge more.

Chapter 11

I don't know how I got home safely that day, as it was still lashing down with rain, and when I parked on our drive and turned the engine off, I realised that I hardly remembered anything of the journey, so consumed was my mind with what I'd just heard.

What did it all mean? Was Sammy simply showing off to his peers? Trying to shock them by being outrageous? Was it a way he'd found to get noticed, to get attention? I had absolutely no idea what had prompted him to do what he'd done but whatever it was, it was unacceptable behaviour for anywhere, let alone at a school, and would have to be nipped in the bud.

As soon as I got inside, shutting the front door finally against the truly appalling weather, I shrugged off my coat and went straight to my laptop. I wanted to get everything down now, while it was still fresh in my mind and I could get it off to Jen and Christine as soon as possible. I phoned Mike too, in his lunch hour, so I could pre-warn him about what had happened before he got home.

He listened in silence as I sketched out what Sammy had done, how the girl had reported it, how I'd been called in to the school and hot-footed it there. 'So, if Sammy's downstairs when you get home and in a bad mood, that'll be why,' I said.

'Jesus!' Mike said with feeling. 'It just gets worse, doesn't it? Will the school be excluding him, do you think?'

'It doesn't look like it, thank God,' I said, 'because he's never done anything like it before. And given his situation, they're keen to take a counselling approach. Though I can't help but think –'

'That this might be the tip of the iceberg?' Mike supplied. 'Me too. So, what did Sammy have to say for himself?'

'He wasn't in the meeting. They wanted to speak to me and get some background before they called him in. Which they are going to do this afternoon. So, by the time he gets home, he'll have been made aware that I know about it too. And we'll hopefully be able to have a sensible conversation about it. I say hopefully,' I added, 'but given his usual approach to talking about anything he doesn't want to, I suspect he's just as likely to lose it. Either that or stomp off to his room and refuse to talk to me at all.'

'Don't let him do that,' Mike said decisively. 'I mean I know it's easier said than done, and obviously try doing it the easy way first – meeting him at the door and asking him to go with you to the kitchen or wherever – but if he refuses, then follow him up there and make sure he hears you out. It's not on for him to simply refuse to talk to you. Remind him that we're foster carers – foster *carers* – not a bloody Airbnb!'

I was struck by the slight sharpness of my husband's tone, but perhaps that was to be expected. The word 'carer' in 'foster carer' said it all really. How many times had it crossed our minds over the years that we did our job precisely so we could help vulnerable and unhappy children? That we were not – and never would be – just about providing bed and board. Countless times, obviously, but I was glad of the reminder. However high the wall Sammy put up, to try and deflect everyone from peering too closely into parts of his life he didn't want exposed, it was our job and our duty to keep trying to push it down. And while I totally understood that teasing out painful memories from the past required a gentle and empathetic approach, Mike was right: it *was* unacceptable for him to refuse to talk to me about the incident at school. 'I'll try my level best,' I said, wondering what form Sammy's reaction would most likely take. Indeed, how he'd react when the head of year called him in, for that matter.

'Or you can wait to discuss it till I'm home, if you like,' Mike offered. 'But I know you,' he added, before I could respond. 'You won't want the lad thinking you need backup.'

Mike was right, of course. 'Wait till your father gets home' were words I had always tried to avoid using with my own kids, on principle – both because it was true – I didn't want them ever thinking I needed backup, because how else would your word as a parent be absolute? It also went against my feminist principles. I didn't want my daughter growing up with the idea that the man of the house – *any* house – was the ultimate boss. Parents – of whatever flavour – worked as teams. And I was very pleased to say it had worked. My Riley took no grief from anyone and her own kids never questioned her authority.

It was something I'd always carried into my fostering style as well. Okay, I might be physically diminutive and there had certainly been a few occasions when Mike's physical bulk and strength had been vital, but key to helping children thrive was to demand and enforce boundaries, which meant respecting our role and our house rules.

'I absolutely wouldn't,' I told Mike. 'Don't you worry, I've got this. Now go off and enjoy your lunch because tea might be late ...'

But Christine, too, seemed to share my husband's concerns when she phoned me after reading the lengthy email I'd sent once I'd got home.

'If you want to phone Jen, Casey, do. See if she can pop round as backup. After the way that Sammy reacted the last time you confronted him, no one would blame you. Don't forget, you're the one who has to live with him, after all. In fact, shall I call her? I think having her there with you might be for the best.'

What was going on here? Had everyone suddenly noticed that I was getting a bit older and worrying I'd end up in a scrap? I could have taken offence, I suppose – the cheek of it! I was a match for any kid and had often been called on to be exactly that – but I knew it was well-intentioned so instead I just chuckled. 'I'll be absolutely fine,' I reassured Christine. 'If he was the sort of kid who might square up to me, I'd obviously do things differently, but Sammy's not the type to fly into a rage and go on the attack. If he doesn't want to discuss something, he'll just say so, as you know. And then refuse to engage further, which I suspect is what might happen. But I do intend to press this, because it rings way too many warning bells. And the last thing I want is to see him excluded from school, so he needs to know it must never, ever happen again. I'd also really, really like to know more about the "why". Wouldn't you? So perhaps this incident – the fact that he's been called out about it – has actually been a positive, because we now have proof that he's engaged in some unsavoury stuff.'

Now it was Christine's turn to laugh. 'Well, you never do seem to like a quiet life, I guess!'

'Exactly. I'll give you a ring afterwards to let you know how it went.'

Both Mike and Christine now happy that I'd be okay, I decided to prepare the tea early so I had no distractions when I had to talk with Sammy. Chicken curry and rice, I thought, which I could keep warm in my slow cooker once I'd cooked it, ready to serve up later. As I prepared everything and then cleaned round, I went through various scenarios in my mind, trying to work out what I'd do and say if I got the 'I don't want to discuss it' treatment. In the end, I decided I had no choice but to wing it. *Speak firmly and openly*, I told myself, *and be led by him, but don't allow him to walk away or change the subject.*

Tea was simmering away in its ceramic pot and the exotic aroma of the Japanese katsu spices filled the house as I watched out for Sammy's transport pulling up outside. And as it did, and I saw him get out and walk towards the house, I could tell immediately that he wasn't in the best of moods.

I opened the front door and he scowled as he approached. 'I know, I know!' he said, dumping his school bag unceremoniously as he stomped past me in the hall. 'We "need to talk".'

'Yes, we do,' I said mildly, closing the door and following him into the kitchen diner. 'So, why don't we sit down and do exactly that? Do you want a coffee?' I added. 'I'm going to have one.'

No, he didn't want a coffee and no, he didn't want to sit down. And as I made my own, he stood glowering at me impatiently. Which I took to be a plus. He could equally have marched straight off to his room, meaning I'd have to follow him and already be on the back foot.

'So,' I said, sliding up onto one of the bar stools, 'let's hear what you have to say then.'

Sammy sighed heavily, then raised his hands, palms facing me. '*Honestly*,' he said, 'it's really not *anywhere* near as bad as what you've probably been told.'

'So, how about you sit down, then,' I said, being sure to keep my voice even, but firm, 'and you can give me your version of events? Then I can decide how bad it actually is.'

'Fine,' he said, pulling his school sweater up and over his head and flinging it across the arm of the nearby sofa. He then plonked himself down on the bar stool beside me, which I liked. It meant we were side by side rather than face to face, eye to eye, which always made this kind of conversation easier. 'Well,' he huffed, 'for one thing, that teacher, that head of year, barely knows me so when I do something funny or silly, she just doesn't get it, because she's not used to how I *am*!'

'Okay,' I said, 'so let me ask you. Is "how you are" someone who flashes their private bits around in front of others, including girls? Is that really how you are?'

Sammy laughed. 'Oh. My. Lord.' he said slowly. 'You've looked after teenagers for years and years, haven't you? How can you be such a *prude*?'

I purposely ignored the insult. 'And then telling people you can get three hundred pounds for indecent photos. That's just "how you are" too, is it?'

'Well, *doh*!' said Sammy, turning and glaring at me now. 'Yes, I could get three hundred quid for a nude, and so could anyone. Everyone knows that. But it doesn't mean I would actually *do* it!'

Since he was still looking at me, and in what felt like genuine astonishment that I couldn't see his point of view about all this, I tried to examine his expression more closely. *Was* this genuine? Did he honestly believe I was ridiculous for not accepting this as a normal part of teenage life? Or was this simply mock amazement, designed to gaslight poor elderly me? Because he didn't seem fazed by anything I was saying, from which I could only conclude that his moral compass was badly misaligned.

'You told the girl who reported you that you'd get three hundred pounds for the photo you posed for. Why say that if it wasn't true?'

'I was messing *about*,' Sammy said, indignantly. 'Would get, could get, might get, whatever. It was just *words*, just a bit of *fun*.'

'To try and shock her?'

'She *wasn't* shocked! Honestly, Casey, you're *such* a fossil. You have no idea about stuff like this, have you? Pics like that are shared round the socials all the time. And not me, obvs – but the really savvy ones get paid ridiculous amounts for doing it. *Seriously*. You've got kids yourself. How's all this such a shock to you?'

Fun? Flaunting your body for money was fun these days? He was right, I really didn't get it, nor did I want to: it was wrong.

'It's exploitation, Sammy, pure and simple. Not "fun". Exploitation. And any adult who'd pay to see your naked photos would be breaking the law. And any *child* – which you are, Sammy, like it or not – who shares a naked photo is *also* breaking the law.' I sighed. 'Love, tell me, how do *you* not get *that*?'

Sammy shrugged his shoulders then returned his gaze to his hands, now clasped in front of him on the breakfast bar. Such small hands, I realised, with such smooth, slender fingers. And with his hair hanging loose in gentle waves around his chin, he looked so insubstantial, and so childlike, that I felt a profound and fierce anger at what had so obviously been done to try and sully him. To use him. To deploy him for sick humans to gratify their sexual needs. But he was only thirteen, I reminded myself, it wasn't too late.

He then surprised me. 'So that's it, then?' he said. 'You want me gone now?'

I gaped. 'Of course we don't want you gone!' I said. 'Why ever would we want that? What I want is for you to understand the gravity of all this and to promise me you won't do anything like it ever again. But we absolutely want you to stay living here with us, so please don't think that just because I'm not happy with your actions, I would ever give up on you. That will never happen, love. I don't "do" giving up.'

Which raised a wan smile. I was then further confused because rather than continue to be astonished, or aghast, or resentful or angry, Sammy stood up and threw his skinny arms around my neck.

'I'm so sorry,' he said, 'I didn't mean all the crap I just said. You're not a fossil and I should never have said that. And I do promise that it was all for jokes – honestly it was – and I also promise that I won't do it again. God,' he said, pulling back slightly so that he could meet my gaze, 'I've been so worried, *sooo* worried, like, all the way home, that you were going to kick me out. *Thank* you. And I'm sorry. You know,' he finished, grinning goofily '– *again*.'

I hugged him back, realising this was the most profound physical contact we'd had. 'Go on then,' I said, when I let him go, 'go get changed and let's leave it there for now, okay? I'll put the tea out as soon as Mike's home from work, which shouldn't be too long now. Chicken curry, your favourite,' I added.

'I know,' he said. 'I can smell it – I can't wait!'

He then picked up his sweater, threw it over his shoulder and practically skipped out of the room.

So there it was, done and dusted. And everything in the garden rosy. Smiles and hugs. A solemn promise. The matter now closed. And that, I guessed, for the moment, till the next thing, was that. But I felt slightly irritable, and also perturbed, moved as I'd been by his fear that we'd now disown him.

But wasn't that exactly the point? Sammy had steered it to that – ended the conversation with it, in fact – and somehow managed to completely flip his mood. What was so obviously, at least potentially, criminal behaviour had – poof! – disappeared into thin air. Had I genuinely got him to realise the seriousness of what he'd done, or had threatened to, or had boasted that he might do, or was this child some kind of master manipulator who had just worked a number on me?

I genuinely couldn't answer that question, not yet, but I now knew, and with more clarity than I'd had before with Sammy, which option I'd be placing my bet on.

Chapter 12

If it had been something of a step change to find myself a grandmother while still in my forties, it was even more of shock to now find myself grandmother to a child old enough to need a suit for a school prom. And that's when even I should really have seen it coming. I guess us people of a certain age often exist in a state of denial about just how old we really are.

The grandchild in question was my oldest one, Levi. He was sixteen now and in just a matter of weeks would need to be all togged up for the occasion. First, however, Riley was keen to do a recce. Some of the boys were hiring dinner jackets, others borrowing from friends or relatives, but Levi's little gang had rather loftier ambitions, planning to stand out from the crowd by getting seriously blinged up. There was talk of sequins and brocade, and of wearing all white (so very sensible), but Levi's favourite plan by far was to channel Harry Styles (apparently not just that lad who was in One Direction all those years back, but also now 'the world's most fashionable man') and have them all wear different coloured velvet smoking jackets.

'Seriously, Mum,' Riley said, laughing, 'can you believe this is the same boy who used to complain if I asked him to change his socks?'

We were sitting in a little café we liked, just off the main shopping street in town, taking a well-earned break between doing reconnaissance in various stores. Riley had already researched online but as we both enjoyed *actual* shopping, the ailing high streets of the land were at least safe in our hands. Plus, whoever turned down a chance to spend the day with a beloved daughter?

Needless to say, though, our conversation soon turned to Sammy. As a part-time respite foster carer herself, Riley understood the many different challenges and had always been a useful sounding board when I needed to chew things over. But after I'd given her a run-down on the problems our newest house guest was presenting to us, it was clear that it was her own son who was playing on her mind.

'I was thinking about your Sammy the other day,' she told me, having taken and swallowed a large chunk of her Danish pastry. 'You know, vis-à-vis all this online stuff you're worried about him potentially doing. Because the randomest thing happened with Levi this week.'

My expression caused her to flap a hand at me. 'No, not a sex thing. Keep your hair on! It's to do with his gaming.'

A Family Friend

Like many boys of his age, Levi was a keen gamer and though I struggled to understand anything about the world of computer games, that was possibly to be expected. In the three or four decades since I'd first been acquainted with Sonic the Hedgehog, what computer games were and what they could do, and how globally the online gaming business had taken off ('It's bigger than all of Hollywood now, Nan!', Levi had recently told me), was surely unprecedented in its scope and speed. No wonder I couldn't keep up.

I did understand, though, that it was no longer kids sitting in front of tellies, holding joysticks or controllers. Everything was connected now. Players played with their mates, or played against them, or played as a team with them against complete strangers. You could even pay and subscribe to watch *other* people gaming – which was a new one on me. (But really no different, Mike explained, to people who liked playing football paying to watch professional people playing better football.)

So, I knew that, when Levi and his pals were gaming, they were often playing against, and speaking to, people from all over the world. And also some, it seemed, who were rather closer to home.

'What, then?' I asked.

'It really was just so random,' Riley continued. 'This young lad – well, I say "lad", I'm not sure it's a lad at all now. One minute he's just some teenaged gaming mate and they're doing whatever it is they do – I'm not even sure what they play, to be honest. Next thing I know, he's sent Levi two brand-new PlayStation games in the post.' She slurped her coffee. 'This was last Tuesday. I looked them up online once he'd opened them to see what they cost and they're, like, about seventy pounds each!'

'So, was he expecting them? I mean, is this a mate of his or something?'

Riley shook her head. 'Only online. Not IRL.'

'IRL?'

'Honestly, Mum.' She grinned at me. 'IRL just means "In Real Life". So anyway, I grilled Levi about it a bit and he reckons he knows the lad pretty well – well, in online terms, anyway. And he was cool as you like about it – saying the lad sent them to him because he promotes their stuff for them.'

'Their?' I said. 'And "stuff"?'

'I don't know. The game, I suppose. The brand? But I mean, who is it? I know game developers are barely out of short trousers these days, but for another young lad to just send him nearly a hundred and fifty quid's worth of games seems a bit too good to be true.'

'So, did you find out who this lad is?'

'No. First off – and probably because of all the nasties we've been talking about re Sammy, it suddenly hit me – was this a lad at all? Couldn't it have been some older guy who was trying to groom Levi? And of course the stupid boy had given him our postal address, so he could send the games to him!'

I shook my head. How many times over the course of a childhood were modern kids told by their parents and their teachers to never, *ever* give anyone online their personal details? That people you met online could oh so easily convince you they were something they were not? I said as much.

'Exactly!' Riley said. 'And just a whiff of a free game and it all goes flying straight out of the window.'

'So, have you told Levi to block him?'

'No, I haven't needed to. I didn't actually know whether I needed to be worried or not, but I thought I should at least make my presence felt.'

'How did you manage that?' I asked, intrigued.

'I told Levi I was a bit sus about a stranger giving him such an extravagant gift and insisted he message the lad in front of me. Told him what to write too. Something like, *hey bro, my mum's giving me grief about those games you sent. She wants your address so she can send you a proper thank-you note – well, so I can send you one. LOL. You know what 'rents are like!* So, he did. And the silence was deafening. And there's been nothing since either. The "lad" has completely disappeared, not another peep from him. Which makes me even more convinced that I was right to be worried, don't you think?'

I did think so; I nodded. 'And what does Levi think?'

'At first he was all huffy with me – going on about me having made something out of nothing – all the usual bravado. As if he'd be so naive as to let "some lowlife" groom him and so on … But when this lad disappeared and then *stayed* disappeared, I think the penny dropped that he might not have been who he said he was so it was a bit of a wake-up call for him too, I reckon. Not just for me and David. No harm done, I don't think, but we've had the big refresher talk about never letting anyone have your personal details. And it really hit home for me just how easy it is for that sort of thing to happen, even to the savviest teenager. Scary. I know my boys are generally pretty switched on, but it does make you anxious, doesn't it? Anyway, enough of all that,' she said, finishing off her cappuccino. 'Shall we get back on our mission? We've only a couple of hours till I need to pick Marley Mae up from school and I wanted to have a quick spin around Primark as well … and maybe that new covered food market, if there's time …'

'Because nothing beats shopping IRL!' I quipped.

Laden down with a new top, six Easter eggs and a homemade lemon drizzle cake (Mike's current favourite), I climbed back into a car that had been pleasantly warmed by the welcome spring sunshine. Going over the chat I'd had with Riley, I was already deep in thought. Though my daughter had adopted a pained expression at my little witticism (other descriptions than 'witticism' are available), I thought about that acronym 'IRL' all the way home. I was old enough to remember when Real Life was the *only* kind of life people were able to live. My grandkids, however, were growing up in a global society that had already created a whole virtual universe as well and could dip in and out of either as it suited them. Which was a good thing in so many ways – global connectivity, for example, the sharing of knowledge to an extent that I could never possibly have imagined – but I couldn't think of anyone who wasn't at the same time worried about the Pandora's box society had also opened. We now lived in a world where people could not only edit the persona they shared with the online world – airbrushing images, making themselves seem different to how they really were – but they could also live wholly different, often fictional, online lives, and in secret, with different identities. Which meant there were now many new ways for bad people to do bad things and constant vigilance was needed to keep our kids safe from them.

Which immediately led me to Sammy and the other life *he* led online, and into which I had no window. What exactly was he putting out there about himself? We had no proof of anything yet, but the evidence was beginning to paint a clearer picture for me. The incident in school – the first of its kind, at least as far as the teachers were concerned – had suggested that he was trying to sell photographs himself and that theory was now supported by the fact that, over the last week or so, the flow of online shopping deliveries had begun to dry up, which surely meant his flow of money had dried up as well.

Which, if it meant what it appeared to mean, was very good news because presumably 'Uncle' Kenny was running scared and no longer engaging with his 'nephew'. But if my hunch was right – that, for all his sorrys, Sammy had already tried to sell indecent images of himself online, and would continue to do so, because how could school or I stop him? – he was still in dangerous, perhaps even more dangerous, waters. And it was simply unconscionable for me not to try and find a way to put an end to it all. But, as ever, I had no legal teeth with which to do so. I could not overstep the many boundaries foster carers had in place. Which left me in something of a bind in terms of how to get any actual evidence and so forcibly put a stop to this particularly grim cottage industry.

My first thought was to try and engage Sammy in a conversation about what had potentially happened with my grandson Levi as a way into a wider conversation about people online not always being what they might seem. It was increasingly clear that he wasn't going to open up about Kenny any time soon, but, if nothing else, it might at least make him think a little. But as I pulled up outside the house, I had a small eureka moment. We had already planned to get together over the Easter weekend, including a trip to take the kids bowling again at some point. Sammy had got on really well with Levi and Jackson the last time, even looking up to them a little, perhaps, given that they were slightly older boys. Wouldn't it be better if it came from the horse's mouth, so to speak? So, wouldn't the best way to approach this be to ask Riley if she'd have a word with

A Family Friend

Levi and have him broach the topic with Sammy when we all got together, teenage boy to teenage boy?

It had to be worth a shot, didn't it?

Chapter 13

In the event, I decided I wouldn't go bowling with the youngsters. For one thing, I really needed to visit my parents, and as the last time I'd been over to see them I had promised to take them out for a bit of drive, this seemed an ideal time to do it. I could drop Sammy round at Riley's, drive on to scoop up Mum and Dad, take them out somewhere scenic, find a place to do tea and cake, listen to the latest round of gossip and gripes in their never-a-dull-moment retirement place (and it really wasn't) and thus earn lots of daughterly brownie points. Once I'd dropped them home again, I could then pick Sammy up from Riley's.

And for another – and the main reason I decided to bow out, if I'm honest – it had occurred to me that Sammy would probably be much more inclined to open up if I wasn't anywhere nearby. After all, I'd always been straight with him regarding one thing: anything he disclosed to me that might either impact on his wellbeing or potentially require police involvement I had no choice but to share with social services. He knew that was how it worked. And given what had happened at school, and our subsequent conversation about it, my hunch was that he'd let his guard down a whole lot more easily among peers. Even if deep down he probably understood that what he said to Levi might still get back to me, I knew bravado, particularly when it came to teenage boys, often helped loosen tongues.

And how, as it turned out. And not just 'and how'. I was soon to realise just why everything we had all been trying to tell Sammy had been falling on deaf ears: he was seeing his situation *completely* differently.

At the point of picking Sammy up, however, I didn't know this. There had obviously been no chance for me to chat to my daughter, though her meaningful gaze at me as Sammy shrugged on his coat gave me a pretty good idea that there was much to discuss, just as soon as an opportunity presented itself.

Of Sammy himself, there was nothing to suggest that it had been anything other than a fun afternoon at the bowling alley.

'Oh my Lord, Casey!' he said as soon as he jumped in the car seat that had just been vacated by my dad, changing the vibe from morose to exuberant in a heartbeat. 'You should have seen us, me and Levi! Kings of the alley. Kings. Of. The. *Alley!* Honestly, we totally rinsed everyone. It was *sick!*'

I wasn't a complete fogey. Having had children of a certain age I'd long known that 'sick' in this context meant fantastic and now that I had grandchildren of a certain age as well, I knew that to 'rinse' someone meant to beat them pretty comprehensively, or master some complicated trick or stunt.

'Rinsed everyone? Who's everyone? You don't just mean Marley Mae, I imagine?'

Sammy laughed out loud at this, which was a lovely thing to hear.

'D'oh,' he said. 'Of *course* not. Though I was playing like an absolute demon from the off. I got the first strike, then Levi got one, then we got, like, six strikes in a row, and then …' Sammy's voice became an excited blur as I drove home, glancing across at him every now and then to flash an encouraging smile or a look of surprise, but I honestly couldn't concentrate on anything he was gushing on about and it continued all the way home and then into the house, where he was following me now, like an over-excited puppy. 'And then we met this other guy,' he continued, 'who was with his girlfriend, I think, and anyway, they thought they were like masters of bowling or something – I mean, they were proper show-offy – and they actually challenged us to a match.

'Can you imagine? Against me and Levi they never stood a chance! So yeah, we did that, and of course we beat them. Oh, hang on a sec,' he said, breaking off to rummage in his jeans pocket. 'I brought the score sheet home so you could see it.'

He retrieved it from the depths of his pocket and smoothed it out a bit before handing it to me. 'There,' he said, 'how good is that? That's going *right* up my wall, that is. I never had any idea I'd be so good at bowling! I mean, it's only, like, the second time I've ever been!'

I paused in what I was doing, which was pulling a packet of mince and some onions out of the fridge so that I could start preparing a Bolognaise sauce. I put them down on the counter. 'You know what,' I said, 'that's the greatest thing about trying things. You know, like you really trying hard with your art. Sometimes you don't realise how much talent you have in something until you give it a go, do you? I'm really pleased, love, and we can definitely do it again. Might also be worth mentioning to James next time he comes. Sure he'd like to go bowling with you as well.'

'That would be epic,' Sammy said. And clearly meant it.

As did I. And not just because it was nice to see how much he'd enjoyed the afternoon and found he had a fair bit of skill at it too. It was because for the entire journey home and since we'd been home as well, he'd spoken and acted and felt like a regular teenager. An ordinary thirteen-year-old boy, getting excited about ordinary teenage boy things. None of his peccadillos, or odd personas, or strange affectations or refusal to engage. He'd been out with a couple of other teenage lads and had good, honest, uncomplicated teenage fun.

It really warmed my heart to witness how that simple prescription had been so effective.

There was no forgetting that glance Riley had given me, however, or, indeed, the point of us getting the boys together the way we had in the first place. Which kind of dampened my pleasure in Sammy's evident pleasure, but I had to rationalise – the point of doing what we'd done was to try and edge him closer to that much more wholesome lifestyle.

I kept my phone close to me while prepping dinner and near at hand while we ate. Riley's text came pinging in just after tea, while Sammy was helping Mike clear the table. *Let me know when you're free to talk*, it said. *MUCH to report …*

I obviously didn't want Sammy to get even the smallest inkling that Riley and I might be discussing him so I texted back and told her I'd call her once he'd gone up to bed. Which, happily, given the busy day he'd had, wasn't too late. So, by eight thirty, having taken myself off to the snug (Mike had found some must-see football to watch so that suited him very nicely), I did so.

'Mum,' my daughter said, with barely any preamble. 'Honestly, this whole thing's giving me the heebie-jeebies. I mean, I've seen a lot, and I'm the polar opposite of naive, as you know, but if what it seems is going on with him *is* going on, it is properly *sick*. And pretty terrifying, too, when you start to think about the bigger picture – just to think how easily these disgusting perverts can get together and get so bloody organised.'

'So, *what*, then?' I said. 'Come on, tell me! What exactly did he say?'

A good bit more than she'd expected was Riley's first observation. As we'd loosely planned, Levi was going to try to get Sammy engaged with the whole business of how easy online grooming was, by telling him all about his own recent experience with the dubious gamer character and kind of see where things went.

'And boy, he was out of the traps like a whippet,' Riley added. 'I tried to keep my distance, helping Marley Mae choosing her bowling balls and everything, but I could see from their expressions and the way they were keeping their voices low that they were soon deep into some pretty serious stuff. And way more so than I'd expected. Levi said it was almost like Sammy couldn't wait to educate him about the perils of getting involved with strangers online. Like there was this great kudos in him being able to explain to him the sort of thing that went on and where it could lead if you weren't super-careful. About all the pervs and the nonces out there, and so on.'

Since I knew these were both terms that, sadly, would already be familiar to my eldest grandson, I didn't think it hurt for someone of his generation to add weight to what we'd already told him ourselves, but it was still depressing to think about. And dismaying to think about my first-born grandson having to hear it, for that matter.

'Sammy didn't get too specific about the sort of thing he's been involved in, did he?'

'I don't think so,' Riley said. 'Levi said he was just talking generally about how he'd come across some pretty dodgy characters in his time – what with the sort of people his mum used to hang out with, and so on. No mention of earning money by giving anyone explicit photographs or anything. I think Levi would have said so if he had. But that's not the main thing anyway, it's what he said to *me*.'

'He spoke to *you* about it?'

'He did indeed. The boys had taken Marley Mae off to get a slushy and he said he didn't want one, and you know when you know someone's just itching to have a quiet word with you? It was that kind of vibe. And, you know, he really does come across as older than his years, doesn't he? Not to look at, obviously. But he's such a bright lad, isn't he? And so articulate.'

'He's definitely both of those things,' I agreed. 'So, what did he say?'

'He just came out with it. Looking so earnest too. Saying he wanted to warn me – in confidence, he stressed that – that I should really keep a closer eye on the boys because there were a lot more "sickos" – his term – out there than most people realised, and operating everywhere kids tended to gather and meet online. So, I told him that, depressingly, I was all too familiar with it all, what with the stuff you saw on the news all the time and being a part-time foster carer myself. And he was, like, "trust me, I know you think you know, but you probably don't know the *half* of it". Honestly, you couldn't make it up. Anyway, that naturally led me to asking him if he'd had some bad experiences online himself. You know, just testing the waters. And he said he might well have had, but that he was lucky. Because he had someone in that world who knew what was what and who always had his back. Looked after him. Something like that, anyway. So, I asked him what me meant by "had his back" and he said someone who could make sure no one could get to you IRL. That means in real life, by the way –'

'I know,' I said. 'You already told me. And?'

'"And to make sure," he added, "that you didn't get hurt." So, I said, "So, you have someone like that? You know – who looks after you? Someone in real life themselves?" And back he comes. Serious face on. Nodding. Said, "Yes, I do." So, of course I asked who that person was. And he came back straight away with "My uncle". So, I was, like, "Your uncle? You have an uncle? I didn't realise you had other family." "Not a proper uncle," he said. "Not by blood." That he was his nan's friend but he'd always been like a real uncle to him. That – get this – in his own words – "He's the best."'

Riley sighed deeply before continuing. 'I mean, really? I mean, *really*? This kid honestly believes the guy is some kind of hero. Anyway, I asked him why he'd be in a position where he'd be at risk of getting hurt – what sort of people he was coming into contact with online, and so on, and he was, like, shaking his head, telling me that he didn't have to come into contact with anyone. That that was "the beauty of it". And I dare say we'd have got into what "it" was as well, but the kids all came back so that was the end of the conversation. Honestly, Mum, the whole thing is too sick for words. Where do you start with a child whose understanding of right and wrong, of who to trust, is *so* completely messed up?'

Where indeed? I thought as we ended the call.

I checked the time. Not too late and no time like the present. I would start at the obvious place: with the child himself.

Chapter 14

I'd had a fair few difficult conversations in my time – it kind of went with the fostering territory. It especially seemed to go with my and Mike's fostering territory since, when we became foster carers, we'd opted to go all in and do specialist training so we'd be equipped to deal with children who displayed the most challenging behaviours. So we specialised in the kids whose backs were really against the wall, those for whom the usual roster of foster carers wasn't an option – those who were often on the brink of being ejected from family life altogether and being sent to children's homes.

As I went from the snug into the kitchen and placed my mobile on its charger, I couldn't help but think back to those very early days and how massive was the change from the jobs I'd had before to the round-the-clock nature of the one I'd chosen.

As a behaviour manager, I'd been involved in many volatile situations because the kids in the unit I ran were often ones in some distress, with the unit the only place they felt secure. And as any parent knows, if you feel safe, you often act out your emotions so every day held the potential for drama. There were always triggers, always flash points, sometimes rows, sometimes actual fighting, but there had always been backup – other staff to call on – and at the end of the day, even if the worries commuted home with me (which they did fairly often), I had my home. A peaceful place to escape to.

Fostering, by its very nature, blew all of that out of the water. You went into fostering in the knowledge that the term 'sanctuary' no longer applied. Not when you had a child with challenging behaviours under your roof (one reason why respite carers are so, so important). During our training, we'd been left in no doubt about that and it hadn't put us off. We had the energy of zealots. And that was still mostly true today. Even though we'd had some intense interactions over the years, I could count on the fingers of one hand, I reckoned, how many times – and always in the heat of the moment – that I felt I'd had enough. Because we *did* have support, albeit mostly at a distance, and with Mike by my side, my big bear of a husband, there had been few occasions when I'd felt genuinely afraid.

I looked across at Mike now, sitting on the sofa, on the other side of the breakfast bar. He was hunched forwards, elbows on knees, still oblivious to the fact that I'd entered the room, due to the oh-so-familiar soundtrack of a football match in progress – the muted chatter, the odd mass cheer or groan, the rise and fall of the commentary.

There seemed little point in interrupting him mid-game. After all, he was down here if I needed him. So instead, I went back out into the hall and up the stairs to have the conversation with Sammy that I knew was overdue.

I was not afraid of Sammy. I had never felt afraid around him. Far from it. No, this was different: I was afraid *for* him. All those weeks, all those chats, all those subtle nudges – had they really counted for anything? I don't know why I felt it so strongly, but I'd come to a stark realisation. That nothing anyone had so far said to Sammy had landed. Not in any meaningful way, anyway. Perhaps because he had been in care a while and had been moved around so much, nothing anyone seemed to offer him in terms of helping him make better choices had hit home. It was probably why he'd always refused to engage with any meetings to discuss his future: he had no real interest in anything anyone had to say. And when he *had* listened – after the incident at school, for example – I felt pretty sure it was only because he'd had no choice *but* to do so. Which was not the same thing as considering his options and taking stock. It was all just so many words, perhaps words he really didn't think applied to him.

Not even 'perhaps'. Hadn't he even said as much to me when refusing to attend that first review meeting?

Hadn't he asked me, and pointedly, what difference would him being there make? None whatsoever. Not from his point of view, anyway. Sammy's sanctuary, Sammy's home, was Kenny.

Once outside his bedroom door, which was shut, I paused a moment and listened. I could hear nothing, but a strip of light beneath the door told me he wasn't yet asleep so I knocked. 'Sammy, love?' I called, 'Can I come in?'

'Er, yes,' came his reply, after a faint scuffling sound, and I entered to see him straightening up after what looked like perhaps putting something beneath the bed. There was a sharp tang of urine and though dismayed I ignored it. Given where we were, once I thought about it, it surely could only add to my resolve.

I crossed the room and once he'd scrambled back under the duvet, I gestured towards the end of the bed. 'May I? We need to have a chat, love,' I told him.

'What about?' he asked as I sat down, his eyes wide, feigning a mixture of innocence and polite interest that I could see through immediately.

'About your Uncle Kenny,' I said.

He blinked twice. 'What about him?'

'About – I need you to be honest with me, Sammy, okay? – whether you are still in contact with one another. If you remember –'

'*God!*' he threw his hands up and slapped them back down again, then sighed heavily and rolled his eyes. 'Not all *this* again!'

'Yes, all this again,' I said, refusing to engage with the false histrionics. 'Are you?'

'No,' he said firmly. 'I'm "not allowed to be", am I? Rule four hundred and sixty-seven or whatever it is in the crappy social services crappy handbook.'

'And do you remember why you're not allowed to be?' I asked, slightly changing tack.

'Um …' he put a finger to his chin and tilted his head slightly. 'Um … because everyone knows what's best for me better than I do?' There was a bitter twang to his voice.

'More specifically,' I suggested. 'As in why Kenny particularly?'

Another sigh. 'Because you lot all think he's "bad" for me. As if that Jen woman knows anything about it.'

'And why do you think she told you that? I know you know, Sammy.'

'Because he's got a crim-in-al-rec-ord. So what?'

'You don't think that's something we should be concerned about? Something *you* should be concerned about?'

'Erm, hello?! Haven't you read my file? And, in answer to your question, no. Because it's nothing to do with me. *Loads* of ordinary people have got criminal records. And loads of *properly* bad people haven't. That's how the world *works*. Plus, it's nobody else's business *anyway*,' he finished, with a sharp exhalation. Quite the speech.

'I'm sorry you don't want to hear it,' I said gently, 'but I'm afraid that's not true, Sammy. It's very much our business when we have evidence that you are very likely being abused.'

'Whatttt?!' Up went the hands again. And the tone of his voice. 'I told you already!' he all but shrieked at me. 'I. Have. Never. Had. Sex. With. Him. Never!'

'But you do send him pictures.'

'And that's illegal now, is it? People can send pictures to anyone they like! It's not *illegal*. Boys send dick pics to other girls and boys all the time. People sext each other. *Everyone* knows that.'

We were getting somewhere now but also, I thought dispiritedly, going nowhere.

'That may be so, but trust me, it is *absolutely* illegal for an adult to solicit and/or distribute indecent images of a child, Sammy.'

'I'm *not a child*!'

'Sammy, in the eyes of the law you are a child till you are sixteen. You know that. And a minor till you're eighteen. You know that as well. So, though you might not think your Uncle Kenny is doing anything wrong, or making you do anything you don't want to against your will, he is doing *exactly* that. He is doing something *illegal*. Something *very* wrong. Something no adult should *ever* do. And however hard it is for you to hear it, he *is* abusing you. Which is something we need to stop. *He* is someone we need to stop. Sweetheart, I know you can't see it, but you are being coerced. That man is using your trust in him, and' – here I spread my arm in an arc around the room – 'your liking for nice things, in order to coerce you into providing those images for him.'

'And so *what*?' he said sharply. No denial now. He had finally, properly admitted it. 'What difference does it make to you what I do? You're not even my family! And so what anyway? It's my body, I can do what I like with it!'

Glad as I was to have reached a place of honesty at last, we were so far removed from any kind of even slightly common ground that it was hard to know what to say next. And the truth was that this sort of thing was as old as humanity, and what a fabulous job had been done on this poor innocent to make him believe – truly believe – that that was just fine and dandy; that it was us poor old buttoned-up prudes who were out of step. I thought of how easily sexual content can be found on online platforms and inwardly shuddered. What was to say Sammy couldn't somehow end up in a worse situation than he was already in? So even if it had to be with him kicking and screaming, and metaphorically or otherwise, I was going to do everything I humanly could to stop that happening; to take him with me.

'Yes, it is your body, Sammy, and you're right. When you're eighteen, you can indeed do what you like but right now, you are a child and our job as your carers is to try and keep you safe from harm and exploitation. To provide you with the opportunities and the support to follow your *own* dreams.' I could feel my own emotions rising and perhaps over-reached now. 'Not line a scurrilous adult's grubby pockets!' I snapped at him. 'To *protect* you! But all the while this man has this *hold* on you –'

'Stop saying that!' he barked at me, his knuckles white where he was clutching the duvet. '*Stop* it! Stop calling him all those things! You've never even *met* him! What right do you have to tell me what he is or he isn't? He's not a bad man, he *loves* me! He takes care of me. Why don't any of you people fucking *listen*?!'

'Oh, Sammy, love –' I began, noticing that his eyes had suddenly filled with tears and now feeling terrible. 'I know it's –'

'"Hard for me to understand" – why does everyone keep saying that? It's all of *you* who don't understand!' he sobbed, the tears spilling over and running down his pale cheeks. 'Kenny *does* protect me. He looks after me. I mean, *really* looks after me. Not like you and all the rest do, just because they're paid to.'

To which my instinctive response was that was exactly what was happening. Sammy, to this man, was no more than a resource. It made me feel physically sick. But saying so, at this moment, was not going to help. I needed to bite my tongue and not let this turn into a row. So instead, I softened my tone and tried to get him to understand where *I* was coming from.

'I could get paid for driving buses,' I said. 'Or working in Lidl. Or running an estate agents. Or any number of things,' I added, as the tears kept on rolling down his cheeks. 'I do this job precisely because I *do* care. About every child like you – the "unfortunates", as I think you called them – who have had a rotten start in life and have no one to turn to, and are vulnerable to predators, who can spot them a mile off. You can't see it yet, love,' I added gently, 'but *that's* how it works. At least in *my* world.'

'But I'm *not* being *abused*!' he said, tugging down his pyjama top sleeve to wipe his eyes with and managing to regain a little composure. 'You don't seem to get it. I don't *mind* doing it. It's only a bit of fun, it's a bit like acting. And it means I don't have to live a shitty life of shitty nothingness. And if I didn't want to do it, I wouldn't.'

'But do you *really*?' I pressed, that 'life of shitty noth-ingness' really tugging at my emotions. The fancy trainers. The high-end aftershave. The obsessive need for things. I got it, I really did. Why did people do the lottery? But what a mountain there was to climb with this poor boy. What Sammy needed, more than anything, was self-respect and validation. That precious sense of worth that he would never find in things.

'Because I don't think that's true,' I said. 'Look at all your art.' I waved my arm around the room again, at all those dark, dystopian images. 'That doesn't suggest to me that it's all a bit of fun. Sammy, love, what you peeing in old pop bottles and cereal bowls suggests to me is that, deep down inside, you are *very* distressed. You might not feel it consciously – humans are better than many realise at keeping bad thoughts deeply buried

– but that's your body's way of telling you that, really, you *do* need help.'

He was silent for a moment, hands in his lap, head down. But just as I was reaching out to clasp his nearest hand and squeeze it, he suddenly stiffened then threw back the covers, scrambled up from the bed and aimed a kick, a really hard one, at his bedside table. Having toppled it over, he then flung himself at the window behind it, wailing now and howling, pounding his hands against the glass, and with truly terrifying force. How much would it take to smash through it and potentially rip his arms to shreds, or even throw himself out of it? I had no doubt, such was his rage, that he very soon might.

'Sammy, love, don't!' I shouted, jumping up as well. 'You'll hurt yourself!'

'I don't care I don't care I don't care I DON'T CARE!' he screamed. 'I want to die I want to die I want to die I WANT TO DIE!!!'

Since it was nigh on impossible for me to muster sufficient strength to pull him away from the window, I was extremely grateful that it had only taken a matter of seconds for Mike to thunder up the stairs and appear in the doorway. 'What the hell?!', he began, then strode quickly across the carpet, grabbed Sammy from behind, wrapped strong arms around him and held him, tight. 'Whoah, lad,' he soothed, rocking slightly as he spoke to him. 'Whoah, now, take a breath,' he added as Sammy continued to writhe and thrash. 'That's it. Take a breath, lad. Now – shhhh – take another breath. There you go … that's it … just let it out.'

They stayed like that for a good two or three minutes, Mike rocking and soothing while Sammy continued sobbing, till he eventually went limp and Mike felt able to release him. His reflection in the window looked exhausted now and spent.

'You need a drink, lad?' Mike gently asked him. 'Case, you want to go and fetch a glass of water?'

I needed no extra prompting to escape and leave them to it. I'd had such a rush of adrenaline that I too was shaking. But what now? I knew as well as Sammy what tomorrow would likely bring. The dawn of the first day of the rest of his life, without a single soul, as he saw it, to turn to and trust. In reality, he'd been effectively alone since his nan died – his mum in prison and not seeming to even acknowledge her son's existence, and that vile, awful 'uncle' a chimera. And if Sammy didn't see that himself yet, now at least he had clarity. That we'd see to it, properly, that their relationship would be severed.

Orphans in stories are always so plucky and adventurous. The stick over the shoulder. The spotted hankie. The merry whistle. The road ahead beckoning. The future looking bright.

Not so much in real life. No wonder Sammy wanted to die.

Chapter 15

Thankful that Easter was done and the social service offices would once again be open, I called Christine at 9 o'clock sharp the next morning to relay all the things Sammy had disclosed over the long weekend, both with Riley and Levi, and then with me and Mike. It had been gone two before, finally, at last certain that he was soundly asleep, we fell into bed and could catch a few hours ourselves. Though not before setting up the stair gate on the landing – no, Sammy wasn't a baby, but he'd still have to work out how to open it. Plus, it squeaked and though Mike thought I was mad, I'd insisted; with both ours and his bedroom doors open, I knew I'd hear Sammy if he tried to sneak downstairs and either do something to harm himself or run away.

I kept thinking of that famous quote by the American poet Maya Angelou: *When someone shows you who they are, believe them the first time*. Sammy had shown us unequivocally that he felt his life was no longer worth living. Only a fool wouldn't take such a distressed teen-ager seriously. Better to overreact and be proved wrong than to dismiss it as his usual histrionics. We were in a very different place now; that bright, confident lad, who had danced so lightly over our doorstep, had now been stripped bare of the illusions he'd clung to. Or hadn't. Either way, even if the gate thing was illusory, it had been the only way I knew I'd get a wink of sleep.

My supervising social worker listened without comment as I ran through everything that had happened since I'd sent her my report about the incident at school. 'Which I'll email as well, of course, once I get a minute,' I told her.

'Sounds like those must be in pretty short supply,' Christine observed. 'Where's Sammy now?'

'Still asleep, thankfully,' I told her. 'Which is more than can be said for us. The bags under Mike's eyes when he left for work earlier were big enough to hold a fortnight's shopping.'

She'd normally laugh at hearing that, as would I, but as soon as the words had escaped from my mouth, I wondered why on earth I'd even said them. Because this really was no laughing matter. They'd just come out automatically – a little levity in a crisis. Understandable. Because we had definitely reached crisis point.

'So, what's next?' I asked.

'Action,' Christine said decisively. 'I'll call an immediate crisis meeting with the managers. I imagine the police will now have to be involved. And without delay,' she said, adding in a rare display of anger, 'Just the thought of this man carrying on with business as usual is enough to make my blood boil. Oh, and listen … It might be a case of stable doors already being open, obviously, but I think best not to have any more discussions with Sammy about this Kenny character right now; don't want to give him any reason to get in touch with the guy and warn him we're on to him.'

'I agree. He might have done so already. In fact, I'd be inclined to put money on it so speed is definitely of the essence.'

'I know. Leave it with me, I'll get back to you asap.'

As soon as I'd rung off from Christine, I headed back upstairs. The stair gate looked a little silly in the light of a sunny spring morning, but I opted not to remove it. Not yet. Because who knew what today was going to bring? What 'fresh hell', as I imagined would be Sammy's first thought when he finally woke from his extended sleep?

Poking my head into his room, I could tell that he was out for the count still, so I risked padding in and, following my nose, carefully retrieved a large water bottle full of urine from where he'd placed it last night under the bed. In the weak light that was filtering in through the closed curtains, the room felt gloomy and oppressive – for all the things Sammy had amassed in the short time he'd been with us, it had no sense of being a space he'd made his own. Were it not for the paintings, which felt more like pleas for help than decoration, it could have been one of those budget hotel rooms where you stay for just one night, on your way to somewhere else. And perhaps that was the crux of it; the way Sammy saw his own life. Had he ever really had a sense of home?

Once back downstairs, and knowing it would be a while before Christine got back to me, I set myself up at the breakfast bar with my laptop and a jug of coffee, to start writing up all the things we'd discussed over the phone. I was still deeply into it when my mobile vibrated and I was surprised to find, on picking it up and seeing Christine's name on the display, that almost an hour and a half had passed.

'Can you hold on?' I asked her. 'Let me just check on Sammy quickly, okay?' Then, leaving my phone beside my laptop, I dashed up the stairs. Not surprisingly, given how late he'd finally cried himself out, he was still asleep and the anxious bloom in my stomach subsided.

Christine got straight to the point. It seemed the crisis meeting had taken place and that a plan of action had now been agreed. They were going after Kenny, it seemed, hard.

'So, the police will be round soon,' she told me. 'Sometime around twelve, they think, though they can't be more precise than that. To take an official statement from Sammy, obviously,' she finished.

I glanced at the time; that gave me less than an hour to wake Sammy up, get some food into him – if he'd eat anything, that was – and get him in some sort of fit state to talk to them. If indeed he would. We might just have another re-run of yesterday. And no Mike in the house to intervene, either. But this was no time for vacillating and fretting about maybes.

'On it,' I told Christine. 'We'll be ready.'

When I got back upstairs, this time with an oat milk latte in my hand, it was to find Sammy lying in his bed still, though no longer asleep – he was awake and staring at the ceiling. He'd probably heard me when I'd been up to check on him minutes earlier.

He had his mobile in his hands, clasped across his chest, the screen facing down. I wondered what kind of doom-scrolling he might have been doing. Whether he had indeed spoken to Kenny, as Christine had been so sure he might.

'Hey, love,' I said, placing the mug down on the now-righted bedside table. 'How are you doing?'

Beneath the covers, he looked such a skinny little thing. For all that he'd come to us with that raging appetite, and a long list of favourite foods, I suspected he'd lost weight in the last couple of days when he really had nothing to lose. And with that mane of silky hair spread out around his face against the pillows, he had a gaunt, almost biblical look – persecuted, hollow-cheeked, tragic.

'How do you think?' he said, but his tone was flat, not confrontational. He'd obviously processed a lot in the last twelve or fourteen hours. But come to what conclusion? It was impossible to judge.

I was conscious of not starting every utterance with 'I know'. *I know this is hard. I know it's difficult. I know you don't want to hear this.* So instead, I said, 'I've just been chatting to Christine, love. Your supervising social worker, remember?'

He nodded.

'And they've all had a chat – all the people who are looking after you down there – and the police are going to be coming here in a bit, to have a chat with you about your Uncle Kenny.'

I braced myself for an explosion, but none came. Instead, he closed his eyes and kept them closed for two or three seconds. Then he opened them again, put his phone on its charger, folded the duvet back and stood up.

'Fine,' he said. 'Okay. Can I at least shower first?'

And the condemned man ate a hearty breakfast … I don't know why that came to me but it suddenly felt so apt. 'Yes, of course, love,' I reassured him, standing up myself, now feeling slightly flustered. 'And I'll make you something to eat, shall I?'

'I'm not hungry,' he said, walking out of the room and across the landing. 'Thank you, though,' he added, before shutting the bathroom door.

Though not letting your imagination run away with you is generally a good thing, mine was off at a canter right away. I knew there was nothing in the bathroom that he could easily hurt himself with, but even so, I found plenty to do upstairs during the fifteen or so minutes he was in there. Though of course the one thing I couldn't do was get into his phone. And why was it on its charger anyway? He always took it with him everywhere. Was this another case of him telling me something without actually telling me?

Like, sorry, you're too late?

The two police officers who climbed out of the car some forty-five minutes later were a male and a female. Which shouldn't have made a difference but it did – at least to me – having a woman would make them seem slightly less intimidating. They both squinted in the sunlight as they shut their doors and looked towards the house. The sun was beating down strongly, seemingly at odds with the dark cloud that had fallen over the Watson household, and my first thought was how hot they must feel in those thick, black uniforms.

The second, of course, was how Sammy was going to react to two uniformed officers turning up and wanting to talk to him, whatever their gender. The sight of a uniformed copper on the street (an increasingly rare sight these days, sadly) was, at least for people of my generation, a welcome thing and a signifier of security, instantly invoking the feeling that, whatever happened, they would step in and protect you. That's the power of a uniform, isn't it? But that defining, unmistakable, slightly larger-than-life presence is a very different thing when it appears on the doorstep, or is standing in the centre of a kitchen or a living room, and particularly so when something potentially bad is going down. And to a child – and Sammy was *so* much still a child – it can never feel less than daunting.

I wasn't surprised therefore to see his reaction when I popped back into the kitchen diner to let him know they'd arrived. Having been sullen and uncommunicative since coming downstairs (perhaps resigned might be a better term), he was now visibly shaking; despite all the reassurances I'd tried to give him, his body language said it all. He was terrified about what was going to happen next and, at least from his point of view, I knew he was right to be so.

With the officers politely turning down my offer of hot or cold drinks, I had taken them into the snug. There was no particular reason to go in there rather than sit around the dining table or breakfast bar – it just seemed cosier, warmer, a less clinical space. Of course I knew that I then had to run through the reasons they'd had to come out in the first place, which wasn't going to go down well, wherever we all sat. Still, at least the two police officers were doing a good job of being sensitive. The female one, who I reckoned was in her late twenties, with a round, smiley face, seemed particularly attuned to how frightened Sammy was and made a point of sitting next to him on the sofa, as opposed to across from him, while the male one, rather older, pulled out a pad and a ballpoint; he was obviously going to let her take the lead and leave it to her to do most of the talking.

I tried to keep things short and to the point, explaining how we'd had to prohibit contact with Sammy's 'uncle' on account of the uncovering of his criminal record and that this had obviously distressed Sammy quite a lot. I told them about the incident at school and the subsequent discussions he'd had with my grandson and my daughter, and how, as a consequence of that, Sammy and I had had a bit of a heart to heart, in which he admitted that he produced pictures and videos for his uncle, hence my alerting social services and them deciding to contact the police.

'As it seems offences have been committed,' I added sadly. 'Though not by *you*, love,' I finished, turning to Sammy and reaching for his hand. He had been crying silently the whole time I'd been talking.

'Absolutely not,' said the female officer, while the male one paused the copious note-taking he'd been doing. 'We're here to help you, Sammy, okay? To find out what's been happening and see what we need to do about it. And in order to do that, we need to hear it from you. That's what we're here to do his afternoon – to take a statement from you, so we have a record of everything from you, and in your own words. Do you understand that?' she added, looking at him expectantly.

We waited while Sammy wrestled a tissue from the packet I'd given him and dabbed at his tears before blowing his nose. After which, he looked slightly more composed. Then he shook his head.

'No,' he said. 'I mean yes, I understand, but I'm not saying anything.'

I think all of us were somewhat taken aback. 'Sammy, love,' I said, 'they have to hear all this from you. It's not going to be easy for you, but we can't help you unless *you* tell them what your uncle asked you to do for him. *Yourself.*'

He stiffened. 'He didn't *make* me do *anything*! I did it all of my own free will.'

Okay, so this is where we are, I thought. *He's decided on his tactic.*

'Sweetheart,' I tried again, 'we've spoken about this. I know you think you've been –'

'I haven't been made to do *anything*!' he said again, putting his hands over his face, his colour beginning to rise. 'I'm not saying anything, to *anyone*! You can't make me!'

'I know how difficult this must be, Sammy,' the female officer said gently, 'and I know from what we've been told that that's not how it feels to you. But it's not right for you to have been ma –' she stopped and regrouped. 'For you to have been doing what you've been doing. Your uncle should not have been asking you to send him the sort of images you've been creating for him. You are underage. And it's –'

'I'm not saying anything!' Sammy screeched now. 'You'll put him in prison!' His shoulders shook and the crying took over again.

I thought back to the conversation we'd had the previous night and what an unutterably cruel start he'd had in life. How could he be anything other than distressed? There was nothing Mike or I could say that was going to change his perspective. He knew this man as his protector, as a constant loving presence. A rock amid the chaos of all his mother's comings and goings. A comfort after his grandmother had died. Not even as the lesser of two evils, but as family. His *only* family. My loathing for this man at that moment knew no bounds.

Sammy's head snapped up again and he looked searchingly at both the officers, his gaze darting back and forth between them. 'If you send him to prison, then who will I have left? He's the only person in the whole world who cares about me. Who loves me! I'm saying nothing to *anyone*!'

The male officer now cleared his throat and spoke. 'Sammy, lad,' he said. 'I hear you, okay? But this is a police matter now and even if you're not prepared to make a statement at this point, we are going to have to take away your mobile phone and laptop for a bit, okay?' Sammy opened his mouth to speak, but the officer held a hand up. 'Because they are now evidence in a criminal investigation, you understand? You'll get them back in due course, and hopefully before too long, but –'

'You can't do that!' Sammy looked searchingly at me now, as if expecting me to confirm that this was an outrage too far and at a loss to know why I wasn't doing so.

I could only shake my head. 'I'm sorry, love, but really, the best thing is if you –' I was about to say 'co-operate' but he spoke over me anyway.

'*Fine*,' he said and I could hear anger in his voice now. 'But I'm not giving you any of my passwords so it'll be pointless you having them.' His hands balled into fists. 'Because I am *not giving you* my passwords.'

The female officer went to touch his arm but he snatched it away from her.

'Sammy, love,' she said gently. 'We don't *need* the passwords. I mean, it would be helpful to have them,' she added, 'but we can access what we're after without them, if we have to.'

I wasn't sure if that was true or not – though it surely must be, mustn't it? – but it became irrelevant anyway, because at this Sammy leapt up from where he'd been sitting, got both hands under the coffee table top and, with an ear-splitting roar, hurled it over. The cactus sitting on it went flying, along with a small stack of coasters, and the table top hit the hearth with a bang and then a crack as the glass snapped cleanly in two. But almost immediately, as if making the point that a bad situation could always get worse, another plant, on the mantlepiece, this one in a terracotta pot, toppled off and landed on the glass with a bang, shattering the closest half of the broken table top into little pieces.

All three of us jumped up. An automatic reaction. And in the case of the officers, I imagined, in readiness for action, neither of them sure what Sammy might do next. There was no fight left in him, however. He just stood there and looked down at the result of what he'd done – the sort of two-second period of suspended animation when a small child has committed some mum-enraging transgression and knows without a shadow of a doubt that they're now in big trouble. Then, as if unable to process the evidence of his own eyes, Sammy flumped back down on the sofa and began sobbing even harder.

Ignoring the upturned coffee table – the shattered glass was thankfully a good couple of feet away – I sat down beside him on the sofa. 'Love, let them have the passwords,' I suggested gently. 'Come on, there's no point in refusing. Let them have the passwords and then they can get on with their work.'

Following my lead, the female officer squatted down in front of him. 'Sammy, listen to me. You're not in any trouble, okay? And whatever is on your devices, you're not going to be prosecuted for anything. We know what's been happening, we know you've been groomed and coerced. I know it doesn't feel like that to *you*,' she added, echoing what I'd said to him before, so many times, 'but you've been able to be coerced into doing those things precisely *because* you've been groomed. Led to think those things are normal.' She glanced at me, then, before continuing. Perhaps asking for permission to go on, so I nodded. 'But it's *not* normal, Sammy. It's not normal for an adult to make a child do things a child would never do. Someone who truly loved you would never ask you to do those things, okay? I know it's difficult to hear but your uncle has been using you. Yes, I know you say he hasn't touched you, hasn't hurt you.

I get that. I *believe* you. But selling pictures of you, for money, so other people – *strangers* – can look at them … that's *wrong*, Sammy. And I think that, on some level, you already know that. You're a bright boy, and however much it hurts to accept that, I think you know it's true too, don't you? So,' she said, when he didn't respond to this, 'let's get this done, eh?' She glanced over at the other officer, who had by now gathered up the coasters and placed the plants on the window sill. He picked up his notebook.

And as Sammy started reeling off the letters, numbers and special characters of his various passwords, his flat, monotone voice and the emptiness in his eyes made me feel more fearful than ever.

'Well, there's one silver lining,' Mike said, as he surveyed the pile of metal and broken glass formerly known as Mum and Dad's cherished coffee table. 'We can at least relocate all that lot to the tip.'

I gasped. 'Mike, how can you be so flippant at a time like this!'

'I'm not being flippant,' he countered. 'I wasn't trying to be funny, I'm just stating a truth. Look,' he said, 'there's not a lot we can do right now, is there? Except be here, which we are, keep an eye on the lad, which we have been, and wait for the storm to pass, which it will eventually. And yes, I know,' he added, before I had a chance to put my sixpence-worth in, 'he is in the middle of the storm right now, but that doesn't mean *we* have to live in it as well, does it? Not twenty-four-seven. We can only do what we can do. And what I'm going to do right now is transfer all this lot to the garage and vacuum the carpet.'

Mike was being practical and pragmatic, two of his best qualities, and he also had a point. It had been an exhausting and emotionally draining couple of days and with another anxious night in prospect – when a kid kept talking about their life being as good as over, you tended to take them seriously and act accordingly – there was little point in us sitting about, wringing our hands while Sammy was fast asleep upstairs. Which he was; I'd insisted he leave his bedroom door open when he went up and we'd been checking on him half-hourly ever since.

I went and got the vacuum cleaner while Mike made the necessary trips back and forth to the garage. He was right about the coffee table. As he'd already pointed out, I'd only put it in the snug because I'd promised them I wouldn't 'give it away to some money-grabbing charity shop or other' and didn't want there to be recriminations when my parents next visited. Though even that was a sad reflection of how things were. It was so unlike my mum to have even said something like that, which made me worry not just for her physical health but her state of mind too. I knew she was in chronic pain; was this flash of snippiness a reflection of just how much she was struggling with her mental health as well?

It was almost ten in the evening now, our takeaway for two (Sammy had refused to eat, and I didn't push it; he was still too upset to have any sort of appetite) long cleared away and little point in heading to bed yet as I knew I wouldn't sleep. And it wasn't just about the police investigation and how that was going, either. I knew they would have enough now to go round and interview Kenny, perhaps even take him down to the station and charge him. They would also no doubt be in the process of getting a search warrant. But for Sammy himself, I knew there would be no similarly rapid response, because there simply weren't the resources. He'd actually have to have a bit of a mental health crisis. Or worse. Much as I didn't want to think about it, I knew that, as soon as Sammy did wake, his head would be flooded with all the desperate emotions he was struggling with – mostly, now he'd accepted that was done had been done, guilt that his actions would have only one outcome: that his 'uncle' was going to prison, just like his mum.

With the last of the big pieces of glass now removed, it was clear that there were shards of it all over the place. 'I can't believe how far the bloody stuff travels,' Mike observed, reaching for the vacuum.

I took it from him. 'Thanks, love,' I said. 'I'll deal with the rest of it. You head on up. You've got to be up at five, haven't you?'

With all the mayhem Mike had returned to – Sammy had cried inconsolably for getting on for two hours – I'd forgotten that he had to be in work early the following morning. They were two staff down and had to take in a big delivery.

He didn't argue. 'But make sure you wake me if anything kicks off again, okay?'

'If anything kicks off, I imagine you'll hear it,' I said wryly. Though crossing my fingers that Sammy was so exhausted that he'd at least be able to do what teenagers did best and sleep for another twelve hours straight.

After all, I thought, as I closed the snug door to keep the sound of the vacuuming contained, at least he hadn't broken a mirror.

Chapter 16

Though I tossed and turned a fair bit, it turned out not to have been as bad a night as I'd anticipated. Sammy was sleeping soundly when I headed to bed at eleven and was still asleep when I went in to check on him at three – indeed, he looked as if he hadn't so much as stirred. I wasn't surprised though, not once I'd thought about it. With all the emotional upheaval of the last couple of days, he would have surely been exhausted. And when Mike left for work, padding around in the dark like the proverbial ninja, I got up too, to check that all was well across the landing, and was reassured to see the regular up-and-down movement of Sammy's skinny chest. He looked so childlike, and so innocent, that it really upset me to think what would face him when he did finally wake. I knew the first stirrings of consciousness would bring an unwelcome visitor; the whole situation crashing back down on him again.

Plus, Sammy no longer had his links to the wider world to reach for – they'd been carried off under the arm of the policewoman. And you didn't need much imagination to understand what this would mean to him. We now lived during a time when people's phones were almost extensions of themselves and not just as pocket computers. For kids and young people, particularly, who'd never known a life without them, they were such an integral, indispensable and huge part of their lives that, as I'd seen myself, both in my own kids, and my foster kids, to be without them could cause genuine distress. And this would be true for Sammy even more than most. Especially now I knew that the contact between him and that awful, awful man had almost certainly not been severed at all.

Once Mike had left for work, I maintained the ninja principle; there was no point in starting what was going to be a long day any earlier than I needed to, after all. So, after doing a couple of word puzzles in bed, and finishing off the now-cold coffee my husband had left for me, I showered and dressed quietly and headed downstairs.

It was looking like being a bright, warm spring day. Which was a positive, though the sun rose every morning at the back of the house, which meant it was currently looking very unkindly down on my dusty surfaces. Which would at least keep me occupied, in the way cleaning always did, so I pulled on my marigolds and set to it.

It was over an hour later when I first heard a noise from upstairs so I put down the long-handled duster I'd been flicking around the skirtings and hurried up to see how Sammy was.

In the bathroom, apparently. I could hear the shower going and, across the landing, I could see his covers had been thrown back.

I knocked on the door loudly enough to be sure he'd hear me. 'Sammy, love,' I called, 'are you okay in there?'

There was a moment of silence. Then, 'I'm just in the shower.'

'Do you want a coffee, sweetie?' I said. 'And maybe I could start making you some breakfast? You must be starving – you hardly ate a thing yesterday.'

'Just coffee,' he answered. Then, after another pause, 'for now, anyway.'

'That's fine, love,' I said. 'I'll see you downstairs in a bit, then.'

I hovered outside for a while, anxious that I didn't really know what was going on in there, but reminding myself that, short of my breaking the door down, I wasn't about to find out, so I went back downstairs to make his drink for him. I kept reminding myself that there was nothing in the bathroom he could hurt himself with, after all, and instinct told me that if that had been his plan, he, like many foster children before him, would find a way no matter how vigilant I was. Not that Sammy had ever shown any indication that he might self-harm, but experience had taught me that in times of great stress, any child could change their modus operandi.

By the time I came back upstairs with his coffee, Sammy was out of the bathroom. He was now sitting on his bed, wrapped in a towel from the waist down, and rubbing vigorously at his hair with another one.

'I can't believe they can just take my stuff like that,' he said miserably, as I placed the mug down on his now bare-looking bedside table – empty bar his rather fancy, and now unoccupied, wireless charging station.

'I know, love,' I said, sitting down on the bed beside him. 'And I know it must be hard. *Really* hard. But hopefully, you'll have them back before too long. And in the meantime, I've spoken to Jen and she has assured me that they are doing everything in their power to speed things up so that, one way or another, you will at least know where things stand.'

Which made me feel bad; the reality being that, in cases like this, where devices were seized for evidence purposes, I knew it could take many, many months before the items were returned. 'So, can I cook you something?' I added, trying to change the subject. 'I know you might not feel much like eating, not with everything that's been going on, but you need to have something in your stomach. It'll make you feel at least a little better, I promise.'

Sammy lowered the towel he'd been drying his hair with and turned to face me. His damp hair, all fluffed up, made him look even younger than his years and those soulful eyes of his, the upper lids still swollen from almost two days straight of crying, met mine and held my gaze.

'You're a good person, Casey,' he said, unexpectedly.

'Well,' I said, touched and slightly taken aback, 'I always aim to please. So, love, how about some grub? I have all the usuals. What do you fancy?'

'I *am* pretty hungry, actually,' he admitted. 'Any chance of a proper fry-up?'

'Proper fry-ups, young man,' I said, 'are the only kind I do.' I stood up, relieved that he seemed to have found an appetite finally. 'So, I'll crack on and get things underway while you get yourself dressed. Plan?'

He gave me a watery smile, which I supposed was the best that could be expected. 'Plan,' he agreed.

I wasn't naive enough to expect that Sammy would be able to just dust himself down and press on with his new, Kenny-free existence. Even though deep down he probably already knew something like this had been coming, the reality of his beloved 'uncle' being arrested and charged as a result of his disclosures would take a lot of processing. It didn't matter how many people told him he'd done the right thing, the guilt would still weigh heavily on his shoulders, and for some time to come. I'd seen first-hand how abused children, having been groomed for so long, wept bitter, bitter tears for the very people who'd so hurt and damaged them. Who genuinely loved and missed them. I could only hope that regular counselling and lots of support from me, Mike and his social workers would see Sammy emerge with a brighter and happier future, even if he couldn't see that as yet. As with a bereavement, I mused, as I gathered everything I needed and got Sammy's fry-up underway, time was a key factor in that healing process.

After fifteen minutes or so, with everything cooking in the kitchen and a place for us both set at the breakfast bar, I filled and switched on the kettle again and called upstairs to him.

'I've popped some of those sausages you like in the oven,' I said, 'so everything will be ready in about fifteen minutes, okay?'

'Okay,' he said. 'Great!'

I was just turning away from the stairs and heading back into the kitchen diner when he spoke again.

'Um, Casey,' he called down, 'I think I need to change my sheets. I'm looking in the airing cupboard, but I can't seem to see any in here … Or …'

Had he had another 'accident', I wondered? Though I hadn't smelt anything when I'd been in the room earlier, that didn't mean he hadn't done something since I'd come back downstairs. 'I think both the spare sets are still on the ironing pile in the utility room,' I said as I headed back up. 'Or maybe one set is still in the tumble dryer,' I added, once I'd reached him. What with everything that had been happening over the last couple of days, I thought, but didn't say, things like laundry had been far from my mind.

Sammy was dressed now, in his preferred uniform of skinny white T-shirt and distressed jeans, and still stood peering into the airing cupboard, his mug in his hand. 'Ah,' he said, 'that'll explain it. Okay, so shall I nip down and grab a set?' He drained his coffee. 'I'm in desperate need of a refill in any case – I don't think I got enough hydration yesterday.'

'Go on then,' I said, smiling at his usual preoccupation with his water intake. What a great market manufacturers of ridiculously oversized plastic water bottles had carved out for themselves in recent years. I was keen to have a bit of a check around in his room anyway. 'Go down and fetch the bedding, and meanwhile, I'll get your bed stripped. Might as well get it done while those sausages finish cooking, then we can talk about what we might want to do today. I think it'll do you good to get out of the house for a bit, and I know I need to.'

Once Sammy had trotted down to fetch the clean bedding and to see to that crucial business of rehydration, I set about stripping off his duvet cover, sheets and pillowcases, and was glad to note that neither had he wet the bed nor stashed any more containers of wee anywhere – at least not that I could see after a cursory snoop around, anyway. The duvet and sheet were just rumpled and a little sweaty, but perhaps a fresh bed would be a good first step towards his own fresh start, which I was determined was going to begin without delay. I gathered them up, along with the towels he'd been using, and opened the window to let some fresher air in before heading back downstairs.

'Any joy?' I said as I got to the bottom of the stairs and headed back to the kitchen diner.

There was no answer. And no sign of Sammy, either.

I turned back around, thinking he might be in the downstairs loo, but I could already see the door to it was open. In the snug, then, I thought. Perhaps to check on what had happened with the broken table. But when I opened that door, it was to find another empty room.

A slightly panicked feeling came over me and only increased when I saw his empty mug sitting on the breakfast bar. Was he in the garden? But if he was, then I'd be able to see him, wouldn't I? With the huge bifold doors, I could see almost all of it, after all. And I could see, from the padlock on the door, that he hadn't gone into Mike's man-shed.

Had he gone out the front then? But a glance back down the hall revealed that the chain was still across the front door so the only point he could have exited was the side door into the garden. I ran into the utility – the key was still in the door, just as I'd left it. But then I tried the handle.

It opened.

I knew it right away: he had gone.

I slapped an imaginary hand across my forehead. All that time worrying that, in his state of distress, he might try and harm himself. Instead, he'd decided to do a bolt.

I had no idea when he'd first formulated it. Last night? This morning? But I realised now that he must have had a plan. I looked down at the pile of bedding still in my arms and caught the meaty whiff of those still-cooking sausages. He'd seen an opportunity to engineer an escape and had taken it.

You're a good person, Casey. Now those unexpectedly sweet words made perfect sense. They were a form of farewell. Good or otherwise, how could I have been so bloody *stupid*?

I threw the bedding down on the utility room floor and hurried back into the hall, then slipped the chain off the front door and opened it. Already knowing it was probably pointless, I padded up the front garden path barefoot, and as I'd expected there was no sign of him hotfooting it up or down the road. There was no one to be seen at all, in fact, bar an elderly man clipping his front hedge seven or eight doors down, but in the direction I was pretty sure Sammy would not have taken – he'd been with us long enough now to know that it only led down to the park. It was the other way that led to the main road and the stop for the bus into town. My hunch was that if he was hell-bent on escaping, he'd be unlikely to be considering doing so on foot. He was a bright lad and if he'd been planning this at all, he'd surely be intending to get a bus to wherever he was going. And where *would* he be going? Surely to the street he used to live on. Surely to Kenny's.

Deciding there was little point in quizzing the elderly gentleman with the garden shears, I headed back inside, grabbed my mobile and went back upstairs.

Unless you know someone's wardrobe intimately, it's always hard to try and work out what's missing from looking at what's left, but three key things quickly made themselves known to me by their absence. There was no sign of his wallet, or the 'man bag' he'd bought when he'd first came to us and, crucially, of the oversized, roll-top backpack he used for school – the one Mike had gently teased him about when he'd first shown it to him.

'So that's going to be your school bag?' Mike had commented, shaking his head as he saw the eye-watering price, running his hand over the matte black waterproof material and checking out the stylish 'cara-biner closure'. 'Looks more like something you'd take on a dangerous expedition into the jungle!'

I shook my own head as I scrolled through my phone contacts for the number of the police station. Many a true word, eh?

Because I was pretty certain Sammy was now doing exactly that.

Chapter 17

There are lots of myths about when you can and should call the police to report a missing person, one of them being that you should wait for twenty-four hours to see if they turn up, and so on, but in fact that's not true. You can report someone missing as soon as they seem to have gone missing, but with resources as they are how much time is put into searching will very much depend on how much danger that missing person might be in.

I had no doubt, though, that the police would take Sammy's disappearance very seriously. He was thirteen years old, he was a looked-after child and was already highlighted in the system as being vulnerable. So, I wasn't surprised by the speed at which they swung into action, taking all the details I gave them and reassuring me that they were on it – and that their first port of call would be 'Uncle' Kenny's.

As soon as I put the phone down after that agonisingly long call, I knew I had two more important calls to make. I phoned Christine first, so I could put her in the picture, and then Jen.

I couldn't see how Jen could help right now though, given the downturn in her current relationship with Sammy, since he held her responsible for getting the police involved. Since then, she'd been messaging him relentlessly, trying to get him to agree to see her, but he'd always answered with an abrupt 'no' or simply ignored her. I knew this because she'd told me.

Her next step in repairing the relationship would have been to simply turn up at the house and walk in on him, regardless of what he said or how he was. Her job demanded that she see him as a statutory visit at least every two months, so that was definitely going to happen. In the meantime, I had a duty to report everything that happened to her, but when I called her number, it went straight to voicemail so all I could do was leave a message for her to call me.

I texted Mike: *Sammy's run off. Police on it. I'll keep you posted.* Then added a whole line of the 'd'oh, stupid me' emojis I knew I deserved.

I then went into the utility room, pulled a bedding set from the ironing pile and, cursing myself for not figuring things out sooner, went back up to Sammy's bedroom and remade his bed; I might as well, I decided. He'd well and truly played me. And there was nothing else useful I could do: from now on it was going to be a waiting game.

I was just coming back downstairs again when my

mobile began ringing, so I pulled it from my jeans pocket and answered it, assuming it would be Jen.

It wasn't; it was the police again. 'Sorry to bother you again, Mrs Watson,' said a female dispatcher, 'but do you happen to have a recent photograph of Sammy we could use?'

This was obviously standard practice, even in our digital age. Ideally, I knew, they would want a physical photograph, or, if there was none, a photo from a mobile phone. Yes, one could be emailed, if necessary, but that was actually more complicated than an officer coming out, as it would have to be emailed to a national enquiry service and would then take time to be disseminated to the correct force and officers, whereas, at my house, I could simply AirDrop it to them.

'Yes, of course,' I said immediately. But did I? Having told them to come over any time, it suddenly occurred to me that I wasn't sure I did. I had no way to access Sammy's social media accounts and the fact that they'd called me suggested they'd yet to do anything with his laptop or phone – indeed, it wasn't even twenty-four hours since they'd been here and taken them away – and the officers involved in the investigation of Kenny would almost certainly be different from those now trying to find Sammy. And time was, of course, of the essence. It was just possible, given Sammy's presumably still healthy resources, that he'd opted not to go to Kenny's but to run away properly: as in head off as far as he could get. Though I couldn't fathom why he'd do that – he had no family to run to, after all. Then something else occurred to me: as the police had his mobile, could he even access any of his money, or did he have an emergency cash fund as well? On the evidence of what had just happened, and his evident street smarts, he might well do. But I really couldn't call it. There was just no second-guessing what a kid in his situation might do.

Which was not a very edifying train of thought. So, I batted it away and thought back to the previous few weeks instead. What we'd done, where we'd been, who might have taken some pictures. Jen, perhaps? His outreach worker, James? He might have taken some pictures, mightn't he? Judging by what we'd witnessed ourselves over the past few weeks, Sammy would almost certainly have wanted some 'for the "gram"', as he was fond of calling it. But perhaps, as was always the case when he asked us to take snaps of him, it would always have involved using his own phone. Then it hit me – his bowling trip with Riley, David and the boys. Levi and Jackson would surely have taken some pictures of them all, wouldn't they? For uploading to their own social media.

With the kids still off school for Easter, I knew Riley should be around, so I called her, and after explaining what had happened and what I needed she immediately had the solution.

'Levi has some, I know,' she said, confirming that my hunch had been correct. 'And you're lucky. The lazy so-and-so is still loafing around in bed. Give me two minutes, Mum, and I'll get him to send some direct to you.'

Only ten minutes later, and with two images safely delivered by my grandson, a new police officer turned up on the doorstep. This time it was an older, thick-set man, his uniform straining slightly round the middle – a man better suited, I mused, to getting photos of missing teenagers than to hotfooting after them in person.

'I'd ask if there was any news,' I said, as I ushered him in, 'but I'm guessing there isn't or someone would have already told me.'

'Correct,' he said. 'But I know we have the uncle's address and that two officers are now on their way back there.'

'Back there?'

He nodded. 'He was visited yesterday and taken to the station to make a statement answering the charges being made against him. He was then formally charged on suspicion of distributing indecent images of chil-dren, and –'

'Don't tell me,' I said, frowning. 'Released on bail, yes?'

He nodded a second time. *Damn*, I thought, *of course he was*. Scurrilous rogue I knew the man to be, you couldn't just fling everyone into a cell without proof. 'And did they find any further evidence?'

'His computer and phone were obviously confis-cated,' the officer said, 'so everything will now need to be examined and put before the Crown Prosecution Service. But let's hope the lad's gone there, eh? Fingers crossed.

'Fingers crossed that's where he's gone.'

'And toes,' I added, AirDropping Levi's photos. Even if the thought of him running to his abuser wasn't a nice one, the idea of him disappearing completely was even worse. 'It seems the most likely place he'd go, after all. Anyway, is this you?' I asked as a name I didn't recognise showed on my phone.

'That's me,' he said, so I AirDropped the two photos.

'Got them,' he said. 'Okay, Mrs Watson, thank you very much. We'll be in –'

He stopped as his radio had begun parping at him. 'Ah,' he said, pressing the button to receive the call. 'Maybe there's news.'

There was all the usual crackling and whistling, and a reliably indistinct voice, and with the officer having stepped away and turned his back to me (force of habit, I imagined), it was difficult to follow all of it. As soon as he'd finished, he confirmed what I'd already suspected, from his closing remark about just picking up a couple of photos.

'No joy as yet,' he said. 'The lad's not at his uncle's. Nobody at home at all, in fact. Still, if we can distribute his photograph now, and get it shared on all the socials, we'll have a better chance of tracking him down. And they're going to do a bit of door knocking – see if any neighbours have seen or heard anything. Anyway,' he flapped his phone at me, 'best get on, eh? Obviously let us know if he turns up here, or if anything else springs to mind. Anywhere else you think he might have run to.'

I promised I would, and after I'd waved him off opened the Notes app on my phone. I didn't know if it would be helpful, but I wanted it recorded because I was pretty sure I'd heard the disembodied voice in the officer's radio saying 'at 37 Englebrooke Road', which presumably had to be 'Uncle' Kenny's address. And as I tapped out the characters, a thought suddenly struck me: did the people at 35 and 39 have the slightest idea what went on at 37? Chilling to think the answer was 'probably not'. And I wondered too – did they have children themselves? How horrible, if so, to know what lay on the other side of their house walls.

My first thought was to jump in my car and drive straight to that street. I could easily Google where exactly it was and I already vaguely knew the area from what Sammy had told me. I'd even driven right by that estate at Christmas time when Mike had wanted to visit a new garden centre over that end. But, tempted though I was, I knew that staying put was the best thing I could do. After all, if anyone found Sammy, or indeed the boy himself decided to come home and the house was empty, what then?

Be sensible, Casey! I chastised myself as I stomped off to the kitchen to find something to scrub and take my mind off it.

The day seemed to drag on forever, however, and I still hadn't heard a thing by the time Mike got home, which was, he told me, an hour and a half earlier than usual due to some electrical problem or other in some part of the warehouse, the details of which went right over my head. But it did mean my having a sudden eureka moment: Mike was *home*. Which meant I could go *out*.

'I'm off to have a drive around,' I announced, holding a hand up to beat back any resistance. 'I know it's probably pointless, and that it'll be like looking for a needle in a haystack, but I'm climbing the walls here. So, before you say it –'

'Say what, love?' Mike asked me mildly. 'I'll bet you are, so you go. I'll hold the fort. I won't attempt anything culinary, obviously, but if he fetches up, I'll call you.'

Needing no further encouragement, I grabbed my keys and my mobile. Moments later, I was driving off.

I knew it probably *was* pretty pointless – I very much doubted that an absconding Sammy, keen not to be seen, would be just ambling round the streets. Much more likely would be that he and Kenny had rendez-voused somehow and, since the police were clear no one was home at 37 Englebrooke Road, had gone together to lie low at the home of a third party. But if that were so, wasn't Kenny behaving in a ridiculously stupid manner? Surely his best bet, knowing the trouble he was already in, would be to persuade Sammy to go home? And perhaps, I thought, as I headed onto the stretch of dual carriageway that would take me to the far side of town, Sammy was doing just that. Maybe, just as buses turned up when you stopped standing there willing them to come, now I was out looking for him, Sammy was already headed home.

Oh, and how much I willed that to be so as I drove slowly past what I could only guess in the gathering dusk was the address I'd heard earlier. Not that there was anything wrong with the estate itself – it seemed quiet enough and with none of the disquieting presence of shifty-looking young males huddled and acting suspiciously on street corners – and I'd definitely been in a few places like that over the years. It was just the presence of that house, among others that looked perfectly well-cared for; like a scab on otherwise unblemished skin. And it wasn't just about the unkempt front garden either – not everyone likes gardening, after all. It was that I knew what, in all probability, went on there.

Knowing I must leave Kenny's place to the police, I had no intention of drawing attention to myself by parking up and getting out, even if I'd been able to find a space to do so. Instead, I wound my way all around the sinuous long streets of the estate, took in a small row of shops that I circled round a few times, then headed back out on the main road towards home.

It was almost fully dark by the time I was back in my own area, still scanning the pavements as I drove. But without any expectation of spotting him, not really. I'd not only not seen Sammy, I'd spotted no one who might have *been* Sammy. No skinny little vulnerable teenaged boys to be found, just as I'd known would be the case all along. Still, it had killed a couple of hours in what I increasingly felt sure was going to be a very long night, with no news.

Having eaten a desultory salad supper which neither of us felt like, the evening had stretched endlessly ahead of us. It's a curious business, being heart in mouth, waiting for news – with it being a waiting game, the best thing is obviously to distract yourself, but because you're in a constant state of alert anticipation, doing that is actually very difficult. I therefore hoped for the oblivion of sleep. While Mike, better able to tune into the football, stayed downstairs, I eschewed a last coffee and headed to bed very early. And when I'd finally drifted off to sleep, it must have been a particularly deep one because when I was first dragged towards consciousness by an insistent ringing sound, I thought it must be the alarm going off. But no, it was my mobile phone ringing. Could it be Sammy? I scrabbled for my phone while Mike knocked his alarm off and threw off his side of the duvet.

Not Sammy. Of course not Sammy. He didn't have his phone, did he? But perhaps he'd found a friend, and … No, I saw – it was the Emergency Duty Team. So, was it at least *about* Sammy? Surely it had to be …

I threw off my own covers and answered the call.

'The police have found him,' the duty social worker told me, after the usual brief exchange of pleasantries.

'Where?'

'His Uncle Kenny's,' she said. 'The police have told us that a neighbour from over the back saw a young lad coming out of a shed in the back garden. He apparently tried knocking on the back door and was looking through windows. Then it seems he appeared to find a key and let himself in. Thinking it all looked rather suspicious, they alerted the police, thankfully.'

I popped my phone onto loudspeaker and started dragging some clothes on. 'I'm getting dressed now,' I said. 'I already know the address.'

'Ah, well you're a step ahead of me then,' she said. 'Because my next request was going to be would you mind heading over there? Apparently, Sammy won't let the police in and seems quite distraught. I know they'd normally bring him back to you, but he's refusing to come out and we wondered if perhaps your presence might calm things down.'

'I'm on it,' I called, aware now that Mike had fully woken up and was sitting up in bed, listening. 'I'll call you back once I've anything to report.'

'You want me to drive you there?' Mike asked once I'd ended the call. 'I have an hour or so before I have to set off for work.'

I shook my head. 'No, don't worry, love,' I said. 'You get your shower and have some breakfast. I'll be fine. Sure I'll be able to talk some sense into him.'

And I genuinely believed I could, too. Oh, such blind faith ...

It was still early enough that the rush hour hadn't yet kicked in, so I was back in the area I'd left the previous evening only twenty minutes later. Seeing it again, and in much less of a state of stress, I could now take it all in better. It was the sort of housing estate that can be found in towns and cities everywhere. Blocks of flat-fronted terraced houses, punctuated at intervals by pairs of semis, built sometime in the forties or early fifties. It had been originally destined to be council housing was my guess – evidenced by the fact that the houses didn't come with garages, being constructed at a time when there were way fewer cars on the roads, the cost of running one being beyond the reach of so many. No more. It was still only a little after seven, a time when many people would not have left for school or work yet, so as I turned into the road 'Uncle' Kenny's house was on, I could see straight away that it would be no easier to find somewhere to park.

I wasn't wrong. Though some had paved over their front gardens to park their cars, we lived in a time now when couples often had a car apiece and those with older teens sometimes even more. I drove the entire length of the road, noting the police car that was double-parked halfway down it, before finally striking lucky at the end of an adjacent street, in being able to nip into a space another car was in the process of vacating.

A Family Friend

By the time I'd walked back down Englebrooke Road to where the police car was parked, an officer had appeared and was standing by the open passenger door, talking into his radio. I recognised him as being the portly officer who'd come to see me the previous day and, seeing me, he signed off and acknowledged my approach with a wave.

'Thanks for coming, Mrs Watson,' he said when I got to him. 'Let's hope you'll be able to knock some sense into the lad. Persuade him to come out, so we don't have to force our way in.'

'Have you managed to speak to him at all?'

He shook his head. 'But he's definitely in there. He's run around and closed all the downstairs curtains. And we've got an officer stationed in the garden so he can't sneak away. He just needs to realise we're going nowhere.'

'Has Kenny showed up?'

'No sign of him at all. We've spoken to the neighbours on the left and they say they haven't seen him since the day before yesterday.'

I'll bet, I thought grimly. *I'll bet they haven't.*

'Uncle' Kenny's house looked even worse in the bright morning sunshine. One of a pair of small semis, the other half of which had a neat path and paved-over front garden, his was home to a multitude of tall, spindly weeds. Tall because they were growing, and defiantly, between wheelie bins and crates and bin bags, several of the latter looking as if foxes had had a high old time picking them over. A cracked cement path led to the front door, which was painted blue and peeling, and then snaked around the side to the back of the house. The air of neglect was now even more palpable than yesterday and as I pushed open the warped wooden side gate, further echoed as various bits of wood and MDF – presumably the remains of various components of flat-pack furniture – were stacked in rotting piles against the wall.

The back garden itself offered nothing in the way of surprises, being little different from the mess I'd already picked my way through. The odd patch of scrubby grass, surrounded by a vast expanse of junk and, at its end, an almost prehistoric-looking shed. And close to the back door, on what had presumably once been a sunny patio but was now a muddle of broken stones, stood a wrought iron table that was more rust than metal, flanked by two folding garden chairs. These, I surmised, had obviously been in fairly recent use; an old takeaway container had become an overflowing ashtray and the beer cans that were standing in a messy group around it looked too clean and new to have been there very long. There were also cushions on the seats, which looked dirty, damp and mouldy, yet each held an impression of where someone had sat. Just looking at them made me feel slightly sick.

'Hi, I'm Casey,' I told the officer who was standing by the back door. I took in standard-issue white PVC, half-glazed and streaked with dirt, with a similarly grubby window beside it. Though, despite the glass being clear, I couldn't see inside; as the officer had warned me, there was a window blind pulled down and a curtain across the door.

'So,' I said, 'what's the plan? Have you had any response from him?'

'Nada,' he said. 'I could hear him moving around earlier –' He pointed up to where a quarter-light window in a back upstairs room was open. 'Moving furniture, by the sound of it. But nothing for a while now. Perhaps you'll have better luck if you try – I'm pretty sure he'll be able to hear you.'

So, I called Sammy's name several times, directing my voice towards the tiny open window, but even if he could hear me, he didn't respond.

After some discussion it was agreed that the police would need to force entry – in a situation like this, with an at-risk child at home, they were allowed to. And it would make more sense to force the front door than the back one, the latter being made of UPVC and looking so obviously much newer, and almost certainly having dead bolts and safety glass.

It was the right call. The elderly front door gave way without a fight and sprang obligingly open, the extent of the squalor in the hall only marginally surpassed by the sweet, fetid stench of long-ingrained dirt.

I immediately wished I'd brought my rubber gloves with me, but I had more pressing problems on my mind. It was quickly obvious that Sammy wasn't in either of the two gloomy rooms downstairs as there was nowhere to hide and as I mounted the stairs behind the younger of the officers, I was becoming increasingly anxious about what we were going to find.

Please, I thought, *please, Sammy, don't have done something stupid.*

At the top of the stairs there was a bathroom straight ahead of us and I could see the open window I'd called up to. To the right of that, there was a bedroom, wall-papered in violently hued florals, with a single bed up against the opposite wall, piled high with strewn clothing, a crate on its side acting as a makeshift bedside table. My eyes were immediately drawn, however, to what was perched on the windowsill, its electric cable trailing – something completely incongruous in all its shiny modernity: a ring light.

I knew about ring lights – they were one of those see-everywhere emblems of the rise of the social media era. Also, much in demand during the Covid pandemic, when working from home became so many people's norm, they were used by influencers to better illuminate themselves when recording films for YouTube and TikTok, and so on. I couldn't help but shudder. It was the first piece of rock-solid evidence I'd seen. And though it wasn't, in reality, actually evidence of anything, I just knew that whoever was using this piece of kit was not filming hair and make-up tutorials.

It was also clear that Sammy wasn't in here.

No, he was holed up in the front bedroom, a fact that became immediately obvious as soon as we realised we could not open the door.

'Stand back,' the young officer commanded, before setting his shoulder against it. He then pushed with all his might, grunting and gurning, and succeeding only to open it a scant couple of inches.

My anxiety was coming in waves now. Surely a bright boy like Sammy would have enough sense to realise that barricading the door was going to serve no useful purpose? That it would only be a matter of time till someone could force their way in – through the front bedroom windows, if necessary. Unless … I felt cold.

Unless time was all he wanted.

Time *enough*.

And the silence was deafening.

Chapter 18

I've been out and about in pursuit of missing children quite a few times during my time as a foster carer and, on a few memorable occasions, ended up in some pretty sticky situations. I've traipsed down many a street, sometimes in my slippers, and have even found myself giving chase. And, between us, Mike and I must have covered many hundreds of miles in the car, trawling the area for sight of a runaway. This was the first time, however, that I had been faced with the prospect of a child in my care having taken his own life. Of seeing that. Of knowing there was nothing to be done. *You're a good person, Casey*, he'd said. If my worst fears were realised, those words would haunt me forever.

But some kinds of knowledge give you strength.

I was only dimly aware of the police officer radioing his partner. Of the words 'ambulance', and 'fire service' and 'upstairs, front bedroom', because all my energies were focused on one simple thing: getting through that bedroom door.

But whatever Sammy had blocked it with simply wasn't shifting. We did our level best, all six feet of muscled officer, and all five feet of puny me, but it was obvious that it wasn't just a case of pushing a piece of furniture out of the way. The door had been blocked in such a manner that brute force alone surely wasn't going to be enough. But just as I was thinking that the other officer appeared, having thundered up the stairs.

'Shove up, love,' he told me, his voice low but firm. And, somehow, this portly and frankly out-of-shape-looking policeman managed to provide the extra strength we so desperately needed; there was an almighty crash and a loud shearing sound, and the door suddenly shifted under our combined weight. Not by much, because there was clearly still something blocking our way in, but sufficient for me to be able to see a bit of the room and part of what looked like Sammy's form in the bed.

With a fair bit more grunting, the younger officer managed to squeeze his way through the gap we'd made and shove whatever had been blocking it out of the way – a huge piece of brown furniture, very old, possibly a tallboy. Beyond that were the scattered bits of what Sammy had presumably piled on top of it – an upturned chair, a bedside cabinet, now in three or four pieces, and two big cardboard boxes, both spewing contents over the rucked-up, balding rug, which I only dimly registered as ancient-looking porn magazines. Plus, a length of rope – *where the hell did he get that?* I found myself thinking – that had been tied to the pipe attached to a radiator under the window, which was now on the floor, our combined efforts having wrenched it from the wall. Whatever this was, it was no cry for help.

All of those thoughts, in just the brief three or four seconds it had taken the officer to allow us to enter the room.

We all rushed to the bed, to the tiny form curled embryonically beneath the duvet. Which was filthy and coverless and stank strongly of urine. A meaty hand, from behind me, came and settled on Sammy's head.

'He's alive,' said the younger officer, his breath slightly laboured. Then he turned to his colleague: 'What's the ETA on the ambulance? Do you know?'

I felt a wave of dizziness coming over me. 'I think I need to sit down,' I said. And did, at that very moment, because my legs had turned to spaghetti beneath me. Flumped down on the stinking bed, reaching for Sammy's hand as I did so, and enveloping his damp fingers within my own.

As with any emergency situation, things quickly became chaotic. Or at least *seemed* chaotic to my tired and frazzled brain. In reality, of course, they were anything but, as the familiar choreography of all those highly trained first responders played out exactly as it should do. *ABC*; *Airways, Breathing, Circulation*, I found myself mentally chanting, as my own dimly remembered training automatically kicked in, ill-placed though I might be right now to use it. Though I hadn't actually fainted, there was concern that I might (I had apparently gone very pale), so while one of the officers got the still-unresponsive Sammy into the recovery position on the bedroom floor, I was urged into the chair that had now been picked up and righted, and instructed to put my head between my knees.

There were sirens, then, two different lots of them, then a new, noisy presence, as two people in green – and young man and an older woman – bustled in with lots of equipment, the fresh air still clinging to them. As I gathered my thoughts (thinking, *coffee – I so need a bloody coffee!*), there was action and chat, and the buzz of various radios, and a constantly shifting tableau of purposeful bodies that seemed to fill the small room.

And then – incongruously, I thought, till I got my still-woozy head around it – I heard the words 'tequila – oh my days!', and a 'tsk', even chuckles. A perhaps understandable response to the profound sense of relief that they had not come to bear witness to a child's death today.

And then, in the middle of whatever was going on, I finally, and *so* thankfully, heard Sammy's voice. First, a groan and then a sob, then a wail that became a gurgle as even while they were pulling him up and trying to get a cardboard kidney bowl in front of him, he was violently, propulsively sick, both over himself and all over the floor.

'You're a very lucky lad,' observed the male paramedic, while Sammy continued to heave and retch and vomit. Tears were streaming down his face now, his every sinew straining, while I could only sit and observe for fear of getting in the way.

'*Lucky*?' Sammy spluttered, spitting long strings of drool.

The paramedic grinned while the other one handed him a wodge of tissue. 'Because you won't need your stomach pumping, laddie, will you?'

Once Sammy's retching seemed to abate a bit, the female paramedic, who had disappeared for a while, returned with a plastic bottle of water and directed him to clean his mouth out by swilling it around and spitting it out. She then stripped his vomit-splattered T-shirt off him, gave him a bit of a clean-up and placed a soft-looking red blanket gently around his shoulders. The young male paramedic, meanwhile, held up the offending spirits bottle. Both the police officers, I realised, had now disappeared. To see if they could find anything incriminating while they had the opportunity? Or maybe working out how to secure the now-unlockable front door? I also wondered if the two parts of this situation were even connected. Would the officers responsible for investigating Kenny's activities, and who had Sammy's laptop and mobile, be communicating with the ones who'd been called out by the neighbour earlier? I could only hope so.

'So, Sammy,' the paramedic said, 'help me out. How much booze was in here?'

Sammy lifted a shaky finger to mark a spot around halfway up.

'Anything else? Taken any pills or anything?'

He shook his head.

'And when did you last eat?' he said, obviously surveying Sammy's pale, skinny torso.

'Not since yesterday morning.'

'Try sipping on that water, Sammy,' the female paramedic said. 'Just little sips. Don't gulp it, your stomach won't thank you if you do that.'

Sammy did as instructed, and as the paramedics seemed now to be gathering up their kit I felt able to go across and kneel down next to him. 'There you go, love,' I soothed, rubbing his back through the blanket. He really did feel like skin and bone.

He lowered the bottle from his lips and I could see a wave of emotion welling up again inside him. 'I would've,' he said. 'I would've if I'd had any.'

'What's that, son?' asked the male paramedic.

'I said I would've, if I could. I –' The words died on his lips, though, because the retching started up again, prompting the female paramedic to reach for a second cardboard kidney bowl. The young one, meanwhile, motioned me to step outside with him.

'You're his foster mother, is that right?' he asked, once we were safely out of earshot in the other bedroom. I nodded. 'Well, to be honest with you,' he continued, 'ordinarily I'd suggest that he'd probably be better off going home with you and sleeping it off than ending up in A and E. It's rammo down there right now and he could be waiting to be seen for hours. But on balance,' he kept his voice low and nodded back towards the bedroom, 'given his state of mind, and his condition generally, I think we'd all be happier if we did head down to hospital with him. And I suspect you would too. Yes?'

In ordinary circumstances, with a drunken teenager, I'd have felt exactly the same. But it was blatantly clear to all concerned – I could hear the police officers talking downstairs, and included them in that assumption too – that these were not ordinary circumstances. Sammy had barricaded himself in as thoroughly as he did because he didn't want saving. And his words, spoken so softly, yet so firmly, could not have been clearer: if he'd found any pills in the house, he would have taken them. So, I didn't want to take him home till I was sure, at least as sure as I could be, that some professional help, of the emergency type, was put in place.

'Definitely,' I agreed.

'Plus, they might want to get some IV fluids into him. He's very dehydrated. Been on the run, the constable said?'

I nodded. 'Since early yesterday,' I said.

The paramedic looked around and shook his head. 'And has ended up here …'

He let the sentence hang. We both knew what he meant.

'I'll come with you, follow the ambulance.'

He nodded. 'Of course. And any family you need to call or anything? To meet you there, or whatever? Get the lad some fresh clothes?'

I shook my head. 'No, no family. He doesn't have any family.'

He looked surprised to hear this. 'What – no one? No one at all?'

He'd hardly finished speaking before clapping a palm against his forehead. 'Of course no family. Hence you being … *D'oh*.'

'Exactly,' I said.

There was no following of the ambulance. In fact, there was almost no getting into the ambulance at all, Sammy being adamant that he was not going to go in any ambulance with anyone at any time. End of. That he was not going to any hospital. That he wasn't going anywhere. That he just wanted to be left alone. And he was very vocal about it too, despite still repeatedly retching. They couldn't make him, he pointed out. They had no right to make him leave the house. He hadn't broken in or anything, after all. But when he tried struggling to his feet and found he could hardly bear his own weight, he lost what little fight he had left in him.

And I felt a little ball of fight rise in me. 'That's enough, Sammy,' I told him firmly. 'You are going in the ambulance and that's the end of it, you hear me?'

He seemed shocked by my sharp tone and then reached for my hand. 'Don't leave me,' he sobbed, clutching it. '*Please.*'

'Leave you?' I snapped, finding it impossible to hide my irritation. I was clearly more strung out by all this than I thought. 'Whoever said anything about leaving you?' I admonished. 'Honestly, I'm not sure you've listened to a single word I've ever said to you! I'll be right behind the ambulance, in my car. So –'

'Or your foster mum can travel in the ambulance with us,' the female paramedic suggested. 'If that would make things easier? I mean, not for you,' she added, turning to me. 'It'll mean you leaving your car here, obviously, and –'

I held a hand up to stop her. 'Not a problem. I'll come in the ambulance,' I said.

With Sammy having given up with his objections, the process of getting him down and into the vehicle was relatively straightforward. A kind of stretcher chair appeared from somewhere and while the two police officers headed back downstairs to sort the now-unlockable front door – which I presumed they'd need to secure once we'd left – I helped where I could, conscious always that we were working around the small elephant in the room, in the form of all those grubby – and in both senses – magazines. Which nobody, at any point, seemed to want to acknowledge having noticed – including me. The smell of vomit also hung in the air, which was growing increasingly stale and stuffy, and I couldn't wait to get out of the disgusting place.

Going with Sammy in the ambulance meant I had no opportunity to call Mike, or Christine, or anyone else for that matter, partly because I didn't have a signal, but mostly because I needed to keep all my attention focused on Sammy, who grew hysterical when he was told they were going to set up a saline drip, as it turned out he had a major phobia about injections: 'Tell them!' he sobbed at me. 'Tell them I don't do needles!'

Shoot me down, but I actually laughed when he said that. I really hadn't meant to but it was perhaps an indicator of just how relieved I was feeling that this poor boy was still with us – and, in any case, the female paramedic had no truck with what Sammy did or didn't do. And he succumbed to it, as it turned out, with very little fuss, causing a small flame of positivity to ignite in my gut: he'd conquered a fear and that counted for so much.

Once we arrived at the big, busy teaching hospital (the one my youngest grandson had been born in, and which I had spent many an afternoon in recent months ferrying either Mum or Dad from and to), it was still only, I was shocked to realise, around nine in the morning. Even so, as I'd been warned, it was all go in A and E. Sammy's arrival via ambulance, however, gave us a fast-pass, so within moments, or so it seemed, we were whisked off so he could be triaged.

This was done by a brisk, smiley, middle-aged nurse, who I judged from her chirpy manner must have not long started her shift. She took a brief history from me, then it was time to check Sammy's vitals, so, reassuring him that I wouldn't be very far away, I left them to it so I could make a few calls and update everyone who needed telling.

I called Mike first, since I knew he'd be worried, and also because he'd be able to throw some clothes together and deliver them to us – necessary because I had no idea at this point whether Sammy would be admitted or not. And if not, with pretty much all his clothes currently in a bin bag, he'd need some clean ones to travel home in. Also, trainers. He'd had none on when we'd found him and since he'd been taken down the stairs on the stretcher, no one had thought to wonder where they might be. And it was a house I would definitely not be setting foot in again – just remembering it made me desperate to have a shower.

'And don't worry about your car, love,' Mike reassured me, once I'd filled him in on what I needed. 'I can always drive there after work with our Kieron and bring it home. Let's just hope you're not stuck there for hours, eh? And, Case, make sure you get something to eat!'

I promised him I would, and I meant it – with my adrenaline levels dropping, I was really flagging now, from both fatigue and hunger – and then I told him that I wouldn't hold my breath in terms of how long we might be in there, as the paramedic's prediction had been correct.

With the logistics all sorted, I then called Christine. Who was already aware of course, via the information EDT would have added to the system, and which she would have got from her screen as soon as she'd logged in.

'Thank the *Lord*,' she said, once I'd briefly outlined what had happened since I'd got there. 'Keep me posted. Hope you're not stuck there for hours. Oh, and don't worry about telling Jen. She went off sick yesterday. Would you believe she's broken her tibia playing ping-pong? Honestly, you couldn't make it up!'

With that added bit of levity, I felt my anxiety start subsiding. But my stomach was growling, so I went to get myself a sandwich and a coffee, the former from a sweet, elderly WRVS lady and the latter from a well-known high street coffee chain that now had an outpost in the hospital – for coffee purists like me, a total game changer.

When I returned, Sammy had just finished being seen by a doctor. I had a little difficulty locating him since he'd been moved into a side room and had now, the nurse who directed me to him told me, been given some anti-sickness medication and a saline drip.

He was lying on his back, staring at the ceiling, his arms across his chest, and with his hand gently cradling a metal kidney bowl. Though I couldn't imagine he had anything left to bring up, I knew the retching sessions might continue for some time, even with the anti-emetic.

'How you doing, sweetie?' I asked him, as I put my coffee on the bedside chest and sat down on the adjacent chair.

'I feel terrible,' he said simply.

'I'm not surprised,' I said. 'But it'll pass. It'll take a while but it will pass.'

He turned to face me. 'Will it?' And it was only then that I realised he wasn't talking about the nausea.

I stuck to my line though, because I knew that to be true as well. 'It will,' I repeated firmly. 'Trust me on this, love, it will.' And I could see he understood what I meant. 'But where did you go? Where have you been all this time? They told me the neighbour only saw you go into the house this morning. Where on earth did you get to yesterday? Where did you spend the night? We were worried sick about you. We –'

'In the shed. There's a shed in the garden. It's –'

'God, Sammy – you spent the *night* in there?'

Apparently, yes.

I don't know if it was the effect of the anti-sickness drug they'd given him, or the fact that he was being rehydrated, but now the two of us were in a cubicle, the small space, with its wall-to-wall blue curtains, feeling artificially private, Sammy seemed keen, even anxious, to tell me all about what must have been an extremely harrowing thirty-six or so hours.

He'd had no phone, of course, and only a very small amount of cash, which he'd used to get a bus, and then a train, and then another bus, to make the convoluted journey to 'Uncle' Kenny's house, assuming that when he got there, he would be given something to eat and drink.

When he'd arrived there, however, there was nobody home and so, anxious not to draw attention to himself, and worried that the police might come there to look for him, he'd wandered the streets for a couple of hours, checking back discreetly and intermittently, hoping for a sign that his 'uncle' had returned.

He had seen the police, seen them knock on neighbours' doors, too, but even once they'd gone he was fearful they might still be searching, so continued to try and kill time, including a spell sitting in a local park, till he began to feel people were looking at him all the time, 'and thinking I was some perv or something,' he added, clearly not realising the irony of what he'd said.

It was in the park though where it really hit home just how alone he was. He had no money now and no phone, no way of contacting anyone. Everything rested on him returning to the house and finding Kenny had returned home.

Once it had grown dark, he felt safe enough to return to the house again, but, once again, he was disappointed. This time, however, under cover of that darkness, he went into the back garden to try and search for a key, knowing Kenny kept one and remembering its rough whereabouts because he'd used it before.

It wasn't where he'd expected it to be, however, and as the night grew ever darker, he was faced with the reality that he could barely see his hand in front of his face, let alone find a hidden a door key. He had a choice then: to walk to the local high street, go into a shop or café and see if he could borrow a staff member's phone, or wait it out in the back garden and hope Kenny came home.

'I couldn't contact him, obviously,' he said, 'because I had no phone, did I? So, he didn't know I was coming, did he?'

I was tempted at that point to ask Sammy a key question. Before the police had taken his phone away, had he texted Kenny to warn him? I'd have put money on that being so, but decided to hold my tongue. I was also tempted to ask him why *he* thought Kenny had disappeared, but that was also so obvious to me that I couldn't ask it either. These were conclusions that Sammy would have to reach independently and, confident that he would do so, even if not yet, I didn't want to cause unnecessary conflict.

'So, you bedded down in the shed?' I asked.

'Hardly that. It was horrible. I was starving, and *so* thirsty, so I couldn't sleep anyway, so I just sat on the chair in there, trying not to think about spiders. It was a long night,' he finished, possibly the understatement of the year. He even managed a rueful smile. 'A *very* long night.'

'So, it's not just me who's scared of spiders then?' I teased gently.

As soon as it was light enough to see, Sammy had then resumed his search for the hidden door key, this time locating it – 'He'd just hidden it in a different plant pot to the one he always used to,' he clarified, suggesting to me that he'd been there many, many times before. Had that continued while he was in care? All I could think of was the profoundly depressing fact that Sammy, so young and vulnerable, and so trusting, had had access to a spare key so he could let himself into that house. That he had spent time – just how much time? – in that awful, awful place. It was all I could do not to think about what he might have been made to do in there.

'So that's when the neighbour must have seen you,' I said. 'Thinking you were trying to break in.'

'I didn't know anything about that,' he said. 'Not till I heard people banging on the front door.'

And, of course, they'd kept banging, because the boy the neighbour had described to the police had perfectly fitted Sammy's description. And the police had called social services and EDT had called me, because there was no way he was coming out voluntarily.

Sammy's eyes filled with tears suddenly and I could see his chin quivering. 'And he'd gone,' he said. 'I knew it for sure then. Properly gone. He'd cleared half his stuff out. I'd thought he might have left a note for me, some food or something. *Anything*.'

'Oh, love,' I said, reaching to grasp his hands and covering them with mine. 'I know, love, I *know*.'

'So, what have I got now?' he said. '*Nothing*. And I couldn't even do a proper job of offing myself, either.'

I half-smiled at this stab at humour, but also felt anguish. 'Don't say that, Sammy. Because it's not true, okay? I'm here for you, Mike too. And, love, I know it doesn't feel like it, but you have your whole life ahead of you. You're bright, and you're talented, and you have the strength to get through this. You've –'

The curtain at the foot end of the bed suddenly flew open, revealing a bespectacled junior doctor with a rainbow lanyard around her neck.

'I'm so sorry to have taken so long to get to you,' she said, addressing Sammy directly. 'It's been manic in here today. I'm Doctor Bannerjee, by the way,' she added, grabbing the sticker-dotted chart that hung over the bed rail. 'I'm the on-call psychiatrist. Is it okay if I sit down and have a little chat with you?' She then glanced at me and smiled warmly. 'And maybe you'd like to stretch your legs for a bit, Mum?'

I felt no need to correct her and also needed no further prompting. I stood up, grabbed my empty coffee cup and patted Sammy's still-clasped hands. I could almost hear my stomach yelling at me now: *Feed me!*

'I'll be just outside,' I told him. 'I'll go and wait down by the vending machine.' Chewing on my sandwich, and much else besides.

Chapter 19

After seeing the psychiatrist, Sammy drifted off and slept solidly for the next couple of hours, time I used productively, since I didn't want to leave him, by scrolling through social media (not unaware of the pots–kettles situation) and accidentally falling asleep myself. Sammy himself only woke up later in the afternoon when the nurse came round again to check his blood pressure and temperature. And as he had long since stopped being sick and his colour had markedly improved, he was deemed okay to be discharged by 6 p.m. Though with two provisos: he had to have a wee, to be sure he was sufficiently rehydrated, and he also had an outpatient appointment with the psychiatric team arranged for the following Tuesday, at which point they'd decide what, if any, further follow-up might need to be arranged.

Having only got my head around the possibility that Sammy might be a suicide risk some forty-eight hours or so ago (as opposed to using it as a tool to manipulate anxious adults, as had been the case when he'd come to us), I felt the responsibility of him being discharged into my and Mike's care very keenly. Yet at the same time, and perhaps without much in the way of evidence to back it up, my gut instinct chimed with what the psychiatrist had felt; that it had been an impulsive act and that he wouldn't try again.

Sammy's decisive, if thankfully unsuccessful, attempt at shutting the world out had, I felt, been one hundred per cent genuine – extremely tired, extremely stressed, and with the house of cards he'd constructed for himself having been so comprehensively destroyed, he'd acted, I felt, out of compete devastation, believing the only option left to him was oblivion. He had, literally, wanted the world to go away. But once the cavalry had arrived – and it had certainly felt like that to me, even though I had been one of them – I had the impression, and again, with little by way of evidence, that it had become clear to him that the real world, the 'IRL' world he usually only half-inhabited, was a different beast to the one he'd convinced himself was real. A much kinder place, a world full of people who wanted to help him, who he'd had no choice but to surrender himself into the care of.

For me, that was a bit of a watershed moment; this sad, lonely child, who didn't 'do' review meetings, or talking about his past, or communicating in any meaningful way with all those well-meaning professionals, this boy who chose not to identify as one of those 'unfortunates', who trusted no one's motivations bar his scurrilous 'Uncle' Kenny and sought self-worth only in material things, had had perhaps the most extreme perspective-shift imaginable. Where Sammy had kept everyone at arm's length the whole time he'd been in care, he had no choice but to accept that, right now, he was very much dependent on us.

The paperwork done, and with Mike having arrived with some clothes and trainers, we waited outside Sammy's side room so he could dress himself in private and I thought back to a Tai Chi class I'd once gone to with Riley. It had been years ago, when she was still in her late teens, and was one hundred per cent her idea – I knew little about Tai Chi other than catching the odd glimpse on telly of massed pensioners doing strange wafting moves in various parks – so I'd trotted along expecting little more than to feel a tad silly, what with all that transferring of balls of invisible energy from side to side and so on.

But there was one part that stayed with me, and it came to mind now. We'd been told to stand in pairs – and with a stranger, which was unnerving in itself – both facing in the same direction, so that one faced the other one's back. We then had to take turns, either to lean back, allowing the person behind us to catch us, or to be the supporter and catch them before they fell. I was good at the catching bit – holding my arms out to arrest the fall of the other person – in my case, a tall man with a little ponytail – but when it came to the leaning back bit, I found it ridiculously hard. That simple action of leaning back, knowing that if there was no one there, you would fall backwards, with possibly disastrous consequences, felt almost impossible to do.

'You have to *trust*, Casey,' the instructor said, his tone soft, but his words firm. 'That is the whole point of the exercise – to trust in the goodness of strangers, to purposefully make yourself vulnerable. That's all it takes, to allow yourself to be vulnerable, and to trust. Only then will you be able to let go.'

And, eventually, I did both, and, I have to say, it all felt pretty weird and scary – which is a ridiculous thing to feel in the middle of a leisure centre exercise class. But it had stayed with me because it had taught me something about myself. That while the role of carer was hard-wired into me – I didn't need a psychologist to point out that caring for others was what gave me fulfilment in life – allowing others to take the reins, man the tiller, steer the ship through the storm *for* me … Well, as Riley had guffawed after the class, seeing me bleating on and stiff as the proverbial board, I could do that bit not so much. I had struggled because I hated feeling vulnerable.

For kids like Sammy, who had longstanding and completely valid issues around trust, reinforced during his time in care, how hard it must be to let go in that way. To allow yourself to be vulnerable when you doubt anyone will be there to catch you. And to know who to risk trusting and who not to. What a scary thing it must have been to have found himself so vulnerable. How compelling it must have been to try and end his life rather than feel that way.

Don't leave me, he'd said. And what a big step he'd taken in voicing those words to me. I could only hope that he could see now, given time and lots of loving care, that not only had his trust in Kenny been horribly misplaced, but that trust in the goodness of almost everyone else he encountered would be key to him finding reasons to live.

It took around fifteen minutes to drive back to the place where I'd left my car that morning, a drive during which the conversation stayed firmly in the safe lane, Mike and I taking turns to make reassuring noises to Sammy about how eating, and sleeping, and resting and so on would combine to make everything feel less awful than it did right now. That we were there, and that we cared, that he must let us care *for* him. All of which he had no choice but to listen to, since he was about as spent and wrung out as it was possible to be and way too exhausted to have much at all to say, let alone mount a counterargument about our motives.

Until Mike stopped to let me out so I could pick up my own car, that was. I felt a tap on my shoulder: 'Casey,' Sammy said, 'is it alright if I come with you?'

I swivelled round, touched by his apparent need to stay close to me. 'Of course it is, sweetie,' I said. 'It doesn't matter which car you go in.'

'Actually, that would suit me as well,' Mike said. 'Because I've got to drop some footballs off to our Kieron anyway. And how about I pick up a takeaway curry while I'm at it? After the day we've all had, the last thing we need to be thinking about is cooking.'

'Good idea,' I said, unclipping my seatbelt and reaching in my bag for my car keys. 'Come on then, love,' I told Sammy. 'Let's get you back home.'

My misty-eyed take on things wasn't quite accurate, though, because as soon as we'd got into my car, Sammy said, 'Casey, is it okay if we do something else first?'

'Of course, love,' I said, wondering slightly anxiously what on earth the 'something else' might be. 'What is it?'

'Can we turn round and drive to my nan's house first? I want a photo of her tree and I couldn't take one yesterday because they took away my phone.'

I took all this in as I switched on the engine. Though exactly where his grandmother's tree was, and its significance to Sammy, were both questions that could wait. 'That's fine,' I said. 'Absolutely no problem,' and began the seven or so point turn that would allow us to drive back to the road we'd left twelve or so hours earlier. Which genuinely felt like it had happened days ago.

The roads were no less congested than they'd been in the morning, but there was a space just beyond the house Sammy was pointing out, which turned out to be several houses down from Kenny's – his own front door now covered with an unsightly bit of cardboard – and on the other side of the road. And though Sammy pointed the tree out to me, he didn't really need to. Because in the front garden was a magnolia, still modest in size, but currently in exuberant and magnificent full bloom. It wasn't the usual kind of magnolia, however, with all those pinky-white oval flowerheads – these were pure white, and instead of the petals all gathering tulip-like and facing upwards, these flowerheads splayed out, making each look more like a giant floppy daisy.

Behind it, the house – another small semi – looked to be well-kept and also, I noted, seemed to be occupied, there being a light on in a small frosted upstairs window. I thought again about its proximity to the very different kind of house that sat just up the road.

'Wow,' I said to Sammy, 'that is one beautiful tree.' I turned to face him. 'Does it have special significance for you?' I added gently. In the fast-gathering dusk, he looked wraith-like – I couldn't wait to feed him up and bring his colour back.

He nodded. 'It's called Magnolia stellata,' he said. 'Stellata means "star". I helped her plant it,' he added, the pride in his voice evident. 'She won it in a raffle, at my school fete. My primary school, this was,' he clarified. 'It was only small then. It's grown *sooo* much since I last saw it. I couldn't believe it when I turned round the corner and saw it again yesterday.'

'I'll bet,' I said, imagining him standing there, looking at it. I wondered how many distressing thoughts and emotions must have been tumbling around in his head.

I was also tempted to ask him the obvious question: *when* had he last seen it? Just how many times had he been back on this street since the day he'd been taken into care? But, really, at this point, what difference did that make? 'How old were you then?' I asked instead.

'I was eight,' he said and I was struck by how clearly he remembered that detail. 'I helped her dig the hole for it ... She wasn't very well by then, she had cancer in her bones and she couldn't really bend down very well ...' He trailed off and I could see from his pinched, tense expression that those same thoughts were probably upsetting him now too. How much had he known at the time, I wondered, and how much had been relayed to him later? I was struck again by how determinedly he had shut down any discussion about the woman who, arguably, had been the most important person in his young life.

People did that sometimes. I had an old school friend I was still in touch with who'd lost his mum to cancer in his teens, and I remembered the form teacher announcing it all to us when we'd returned from the summer holidays. How we were advised to treat him gently and to comfort him when he cried. I remembered especially how he didn't – not ever. And I recalled a conversation we'd had two decades or so later and how he'd said that his dad believed it would be best for both his children – less upsetting for them, he'd thought, and definitely for him – if they didn't mention her at all. It had, he told me – this business of having to push away all those memories, so his father didn't cry – messed him up in the head for many years.

I couldn't imagine Sammy's first foster carer behaving similarly, because it was hard-wired into us that, in almost all cases, rummaging in that mental memory box and recalling, and talking about, the dead loved one was vital to kids' emotional health, however upsetting. But perhaps Sammy, already scarred by his mother's neglect and disappearance, had made up his own mind that, once his grandmother was gone, much the best thing was to forget her.

Except clearly, he hadn't. And couldn't. And shouldn't.

'Well, let's get out and get some pictures for you now, shall we?' I said, smiling at him as I unclipped my seatbelt and pulled my phone out of my bag. 'It's nice to see that whoever lives there now has taken such good care of it, isn't it?'

'It's beautiful, isn't it?' Sammy said as we stood and studied the tree more closely.

I clicked away on my phone, taking multiple shots from all kinds of angles, trying to get some really good pictures we could print off for him. And seeing the emotion on his face as he watched me doing my nature photography bit (heaven knows what the current residents might have thought if they'd glanced out the front and seen me), I had another thought.

'I know you were young when your nan died, love,' I said, 'but did you get to keep anything of hers? You know, like a memento? Some jewellery of hers? Something to remember her by?'

The light faded from his face and I could see my question had caused him some pain. 'Nothing,' he said, tears springing to his eyes. 'I don't think anyone even thought to ask me. They just gave me a photo they found – the social services people did – and I was too young to ask. I just thought that was all I was allowed. One of my friends whose dad died has some of his ashes in a little glass jar,' he added, the thought obviously just coming to him. 'But I don't have anything, just that one photo.'

He'd stopped speaking so I stopped taking pictures and turned to face him. I could see his chin dimpling and wobbling as he struggled with another bout of tears. 'It's not just like she's gone, it's almost like she never even *existed*,' he managed to get out before breaking down into a paroxysm of sobbing.

'Oh, darling, come here,' I said, pulling him into my arms and embracing him tightly, once again struck by how he seemed to be all skin and bone. I rocked him gently for some time, just as Mike had done a few days ago.

Good Lord, I thought, *such a lot has happened in such a short space of time*.

'Sweetheart,' I said eventually, 'I know she's no longer here, but, you know, she *is* – in another way, she's always going to be with you. In your heart, in your mind, in all the memories you have of her, in all the things she taught you and told you – like the name of that tree, for example – in all the ways she made you feel loved.' I pulled back, released him and placed my hand on his chest instead. 'She will be in here, always with you, and cheering you on. And though I didn't know her, I don't need to, to be able to tell just how much she loved you. And, wherever she is now, just how *proud* she is of you. You've come through so much, sweetheart, and all by yourself. And you know what?' I said, the idea having just taken shape, 'I will see what else I can find – or I can do – so you have more than just that photograph to remember her by.'

'Like what?' he said, brushing tears from his cheeks now. 'I mean, how? What can *you* do?'

I had no idea, of course, but there would have to be *something*. There would surely, at the very least, be some channel to Sammy's mother. Or something on his file. Or someone, somewhere, who'd have some small thing, surely? Even – and I shuddered to think of it, obviously – in the hands of that bloody monster who'd until very recently been resident down the road. And if there weren't any mementoes, then some memorial to her. So, no, I didn't know what exactly, but there would be something we could do. Even a seedhead from the tree we were standing in front of, so another, with its exact same DNA, could be grown. We could even grow it together, couldn't we?

I knew I should feel sad about the plight of this poor lad, but, instead, in that moment, I felt oddly buoyant. That this poor, wretched boy's life was finally starting.

I slipped my phone in my pocket and put an arm back around him.

'Lots, love,' I told him firmly. '*Lots*.'

Chapter 20

Unsurprisingly, Sammy slept till almost noon the next day and I was happy for him to do so. I still couldn't help myself though; having checked on him multiple times overnight, barely getting any sleep myself, my regime that morning was to do half-hourly checks. In between times, I concentrated on getting everything down about the previous day's unbelievable events, which was the biggest reporting task I'd undertaken in a long time. It also felt unbelievable that only a little over twenty-four hours had passed since that call had come in from EDT.

Perhaps also unsurprisingly, within minutes of my email going off to both Christine and Jen, my phone sprang to life.

'To use a phrase I've heard you use a hundred times,' Christine started, 'what a bloody day you've had! Actually, what a bloody few days, to be more accurate.'

I laughed. 'What a few bloody days indeed,' I said, 'and, yes, for sure, yesterday. To be honest, I'm surprised I don't have the banging headache to prove it.'

'Bless you, I don't doubt it. And let's hope one doesn't arrive. And how is Sammy, or is it too soon to know?'

'A bit broken,' I said, 'but I think this will be the start of his recovery. A long road ahead for sure, but when you hit rock bottom, there's only one way to go, right?'

'Let's hope so,' Christine said, sighing audibly. 'What a nasty piece of work that Kenny must have been, must *still* be. No, *is*. They haven't caught him yet, by the way, but they will. I hope they find enough evidence to throw away the bloody key!'

'Well, he will be going to jail for sure,' I said, remembering, unpleasantly, the ring light I'd seen on that bedroom windowsill and the piles of porn mags that had spewed from that fallen cardboard box. 'Because I'm confident they'll find everything they need in that horrible, sordid house. It's hard to believe this stuff happens right under the noses of all the neighbours, isn't it? Oh, by the way, speaking of which, did you see in my report that the hospital want Sammy to see their mental health team? The appointment is on Tuesday, so it isn't a school day, but I'm going to keep him off school anyway. If that's okay, that is?'

'Of course,' Christine said. 'No way will he be up for school. But leave all that to me, you have enough to do. I'll phone his head of year and tell her as much as I can.

And yes, I did know. I read your whole report and that's a big plus from our point of view as well, to be honest, because the PIPA team are up to their eyeballs just now so it could have been weeks before we got Sammy a one-to-one with them.'

Christine did all her supervising social worker duties next, thanking me for such a detailed report and for the work we were putting in with Sammy, and asking how me and Mike were holding up ourselves, did we need any extra help, and so on. To which I answered fine, and that, no, we really didn't.

'Are you *sure*, Casey?' she asked me earnestly. 'No one could blame you if you needed a couple of days' respite.'

'I'm fine,' I insisted. 'I promise. I'm a little tired, of course, but I'm honestly feeling okay. I'm just so glad everything has finally come out and that monster is going to get what he deserves. I'm feeling energised, actually, because Sammy can now move on with his life, can't he? Oh, but there is one thing,' I added, 'because I'm not sure where to start with it.'

'Which is?'

I went on to explain about Sammy's grandmother's tree and how upset he had been when he'd seen it again, realising he had nothing to remember her by except a single photograph. 'Which I'm hoping he's going to show me today,' I went on. 'But, you know, it really struck me – how can there not have been anything passed on to him? When she died, what would have happened to all her personal effects? I mean, who arranged her funeral? If she even had one, that is. I know more and more people these days opt for that direct cremation set-up, don't they? And if she had no family, and with Sammy's mum being in prison – assuming she was at the time? – and with presumably little money … Is this something you can look into and maybe shed a bit of light on? I had this mad hope that her ashes might be stored somewhere or something. I know it's a long shot but …'

'I can answer one of those questions right now,' Christine said. 'I've been reading Sammy's file and it seems his nan was cremated. I even have the name of the cemetery and the funeral directors. Turns out it was none other than Uncle Kenny who organised the cremation, can you believe?'

'Well, yes, I guess he would, if they were as close as we've been told. God, if she only knew, eh?'

'Indeed. Things might have worked out very differently. But that's all water under the bridge now, I guess. And as for any ashes, I can certainly find out. As Sammy's legal guardians, I'm pretty sure we have the right to make enquiries. Leave it with me and I'll see what I can do. It's possible Kenny had them, but equally they might still have them in storage.'

'And what about other stuff? What would have happened to her personal effects? It seems unlikely that no one thought there might be things Sammy might have wanted?'

'They probably would have,' Christine agreed, 'but I'm guessing anything she had would have been left to her daughter. Though if she was in prison when the nan died, who knows what might have happened? It could be that the council brought a house clearance firm in. But, again, let me see what I can find out. Though don't get any hopes up on that front. Since Sammy's first carers left fostering a good while ago now, it's possible we won't be able to find anything out there. But I will do my best, I promise.'

'I know you will,' I told her. 'And I won't mention anything to Sammy just yet, obviously. Plus, if all this comes to nothing, I also have a plan B.'

'Which is?'

I told her about my plan to wait until autumn then embark on a mission to gather some seedheads from Sammy's nan's tree. 'Seriously,' I said. 'I had Mike look it up. Magnolias aren't hard to propagate from seed, apparently. And it will be something Sammy and I can do together, won't it?'

Christine laughed. 'The things you think of! A gold star for Mrs Watson!'

I didn't know about that – it was actually quite a kooky idea. Was a thirteen-year-old lad really going to want to go through life accompanied by a tree in a pot? But we could plant it in our garden and at least it would be something – you could only do what you could do, after all.

It was Sammy's immediate future, however, that was my main priority. And though when he eventually appeared, at one thirty, his colour was better, it hit me anew just how much he had changed. Yes, he was skinnier – that was all too obvious – but I could sort that by feeding him. Ditto the dark circles under his eyes, which could be improved over time, with lots of rest.

No, the change was subtler, though plain as day to me. The boy who'd bounced across our doorstep back in January, waving his sunshine yellow scarf, had completely lost his spark. And it would take more than a fry-up and free rein with the remote to bring it back.

'You okay, sweetheart?' I asked. 'Are you hungry?'

'I am,' he said, smiling weakly. Then, obviously keen to make an effort, 'My stomach thinks my throat's been cut.'

I'd never heard that expression before but it's meaning was obvious. As it was clear he was trying to be funny, I duly laughed as I opened the fridge.

'Bacon, sausages, eggs and beans, then?' I asked. The same menu, I realised, that I'd been in the process of rustling up when he'd absconded. In fact, the key part of the ruse he'd engineered to enable him to.

He might have lost his spark but he hadn't lost his smarts. 'Yes, please,' he said and then managed a rueful grin. 'Don't worry,' he said. 'Today, I'm going to eat it. I mean, it's not like I have anywhere to go, is it?'

And there it was. The stark reality that Sammy was speaking the truth. With Kenny out of the picture now, what had been clear for us for a while was an unescapable truth for Sammy now as well, so my job now was to convince him that life would somehow get better and that he needed to trust those of us who were trying to help him. For now, though, I would cook, I would smile, and, determined to outshine any darkness he felt today, I would turn up the cheesy music on my Alexa.

'Feel free to dance,' I told him, happy to see his eye roll and head shake as he climbed up onto a stool by the breakfast bar to watch me make the meal for us. We both knew he was in no mood for dancing. But he was, it seemed, in the mood for talking.

'I still can't believe he'd just abandon me like that,' he said, entirely without prompting, while I was busy turning the sausages in the pan. 'I mean, I have to, because he did, but still …' He sighed. 'I wonder where he is? I mean, where would he even *go*?'

I had no idea. I knew all about the old adage of honour among thieves, but would that be the case here? Might he be holed up somewhere, sofa-surfing with one of his kind? I was more concerned that Sammy, having slept, and having reflected, might be worrying about him. After all, when you are badly let down by someone you believe would never do so, it's often easier to find excuses for them than to face the truth. Almost like gaslighting yourself. It was a worry he soon confirmed: 'I mean, suppose he's been trying to contact me all this time? I don't have my phone, do I?'

I kept my back to him, busying myself at the hob. What to say to this unexpected disclosure? Was now the time to ask the question I'd opted not to in the hospital?

To establish if Sammy *had* tipped him off about the police? 'Had you been texting him then?' I plumped for, keeping my tone light rather than pointed.

'A bit,' he admitted. 'Just you know, when I knew about the police going after him. I mean, I couldn't not. I knew I wasn't allowed to, but I just felt I *had* to, you know?'

It was impossible to agree with that truthfully, so I didn't. But his loyalty to this evil man was a solid, well-built structure – of course it was. He'd been a big, important part of Sammy's childhood so I knew I couldn't knock it down with just a couple of well-chosen words. But I said them anyway, because one brick at a time was better than nothing.

'Do you have read receipts on your phone, love?' I asked, now turning to face him. He nodded. And, smart boy that he was, he got my inference right away.

'Yes,' he said flatly. 'And yes, he'd read them all. And never answered. Not anything. Not even a thumbs-up emoji to let me know he'd got them. But what if he *couldn't* message me back? What if by the time he'd worked out what to do, tell me where he was going, he did try? And *couldn't*? Because the police took my phone?'

I could see how much he wanted this theory to be true. His eyes were searching mine now for some hint that I saw his argument as being feasible. Which of course it was. It could have happened *exactly* like that. And in the fullness of time, perhaps the police would be able to confirm it one way or the other. In the here and now, however, that wasn't really the point. It wouldn't be helpful, I realised, to insist that his 'uncle' cared not a jot about what happened to him – it would just poke that loyalty button further.

'That could have happened,' I conceded. 'And he knew he'd been warned not to contact you, so that would have been on his mind too. But you know,' I pressed on, 'it's all water under the bridge now. Look, love,' I said gently, 'the thing is that everyone knows how much Kenny meant to you. Even though we knew the relationship was wrong, we all knew and understood. That might sound weird to you, because of what we now know about him, but it's true. And I also understand that it's not going to be easy for you to just switch off your feelings. And perhaps you're right. Perhaps he *does* feel bad about it all. About running away like that and abandoning you. About not leaving you a note or anything. But perhaps, when it came to it, he just felt he had to make that choice. Perhaps he knew you'd be better off without him.'

I paused, trying to judge if what I said next would upset him further, but in for a penny and all that. It would at least give him pause for thought. 'Sweetheart, I know we've covered this ground before, but I think it's worth repeating. Kenny earned his living doing something that's not only illegal but also …' I paused again. Was I right to try and reframe the narrative for him to make it all feel more palatable? So he could pity the man rather than hate him? Perhaps not, but what was there to lose? '… but also sick,' I went on. 'I think *he* is sick. That's the truth of it. To ask the things he asked of you is sick. Morally sick. And, don't forget, he might well have been asking them of other children too.'

I was about to say more but Sammy's anguished expression stopped me.

'What, love?'

Silence. His hands were clasped in front of him on the breakfast bar and he studied them for some seconds.

'Sammy, tell me.'

He looked up at me then, clearly undecided about sharing whatever it was that was troubling him. 'He did.' His voice was barely a whisper.

'You knew he'd asked other children to make pictures and films for him?'

He looked scared now, then shook his head. 'No,' he said. 'I mean, I don't know. He just asked if … you know …'

The penny dropped. Of *course*. 'Sammy, did Kenny ask *you* if you could suggest any other children, who might –'

'I never did!' he interrupted, his tone indignant.

'No, of *course* you didn't, love. I would never think you did, but –'

'But he used to ask me. You know, like, since I went into Year 9 and that. Like, did any of my mates fancy earning a few quid?'

It was impossible to feel any more sickened by this man than I did already and this, surely, was par for the course for these characters: reel them in, make it all seem normal, get them to recruit. It was like it was out of the Epstein bloody playbook. So, I wasn't shocked. In fact, I was encouraged by this admission.

'But I never *ever* did,' Sammy said again. 'I would *never*.'

'I know that, love. Of *course* you wouldn't. I would never think that of you.'

I let the thought settle while I added eggs to the frying pan. So, on one level, without question, Sammy had known it was wrong. He had refused to cross that line. It was a heartening thing to know.

'He knew I was going to go there,' he said suddenly, changing tack completely. 'To his house. That's why he hid the key somewhere else, wasn't it? So I couldn't get in, so I couldn't *see* …'

I wasn't sure where Sammy's train of thought was going now but it was clearly galloping along. Painful realities beginning to fall into place.

'See what?' I asked.

'Stuff in there. I could see through the back down-stairs window, toys and stuff. Why would he have those?'

It was a question I could see he didn't expect me to answer. God, I hoped they found the guy, and very soon. But it was perhaps this realisation by Sammy – that he wasn't special to Kenny, that he was just one of a number – that would do the greatest good in opening his eyes.

I was torn now. The food was ready, the conversation far from over, but perhaps it was enough soul-searching for today. 'I know,' I said, even though it was a room I'd barely glanced in. 'It was a pretty grim place to find myself in, believe me.'

'I saw you,' he said then, surprising me again. 'I saw you driving down the road and I nearly called out to you. You know, while I was hiding. I nearly did –'

'Oh, love, I wish you had,' I said. 'I wish I'd seen *you*.'

He frowned, then smiled ruefully at me. 'I should've, shouldn't I?'

'Yes, you should have. But what's done is done, eh? And we are where we are. You're back *now*, which is all that matters. Now how's about we eat this very belated breakfast?'

Sammy nodded. 'I am *so* hungry. My stomach doesn't just think my throat has been cut, it feels like my whole head's run away to Timbuktu.'

'Hank Marvin,' I said.

'Hank what?'

'You're Hank Marvin. Starvin'. Something one of our foster children from a long time ago used to say. Right then, let's get this on some plates, shall we? Enough talking, time for eating.'

Sammy smiled and I could see he was done with talking too. 'Hank Marvin. You're so funny, Casey,' he said.

* * *

A Family Friend

The next few days were very quiet, Sammy spending a lot of time painting. And a similar amount watching movies on TV and also sunbathing in the garden, to 'get his tan on'. Which was fine by me. I was keen not to push for anything different; I knew that this period of reflection, without the distractions of school or days out, was very important for him. His whole world had been turned upside down and he would need lots of time to now find himself again and to work out who he could be without Kenny's influence – a task made immeasurably easier, I reckoned, without the constant siren call of the internet and social media. Most tellingly, as Mike had pointed out over the weekend, he hadn't wet the bed, or filled a bottle with urine, since the day he'd come home.

'Which makes you realise,' he'd added, 'just how distressed the poor lad's been. And to know that was the only way he could let us know how he was feeling … that he couldn't *tell* anyone. It's so bloody sad, isn't it?'

I agreed that it was. But that was hopefully about to change because, on the Tuesday, it was time to return to the hospital, for Sammy's follow-up appointment with the psychiatrist. For which, for the first time in days, he'd made a big sartorial effort, opting for an as yet unworn white T-shirt, his favourite skinny jeans and faux-leather jacket combo, and with one of his bright cotton scarves wrapped around his neck.

If ever clothing was armour, I thought, *this was it.*

'I'm proper nervous,' Sammy said as we headed down the seemingly never-ending corridor. 'What kind of stuff do you think she'll ask me?'

'I'm not sure, kiddo,' I said, truthfully, 'but I do know that these sessions are designed to be comfortable for you, so everything will be at a pace you're happy with. So, if the doctor asks you anything you really don't want to answer, you can say so. But, love,' I counselled, 'try to open up if you can. Bottling things up will only hurt you in the long run, so it's much better to be open and honest if you can. Never forget, all the doctor wants is to help you.'

Sammy nodded but I could still see the anxiety in his expression, so it was with great relief that when he was called, it was by a young-looking woman with warm, grey-green eyes – and not the grizzled older man most people brought to mind when they heard the word 'psychiatrist'.

'I'm Doctor Summers,' she said when she'd identified us from my raised hand. 'Mrs Watson, yes?' she added as she led the way into her consulting room round the corner. 'And you must be Sammy? Wow, I *love* your jacket! Where'd you get it?'

I could have kissed her. It was just what had been needed to ease Sammy's nerves. Though, instead of doing that, I took the seat outside the door she pointed out for me, one of a row of three, and where I was apparently to wait till their session was over. Or, at least, return to: 'An hour, yes?' I asked her.

The doctor smiled and nodded. 'So, you were saying, Sammy?' she went on, as they headed through the door.

'Oh, it's just a cheap one from Shein,' he said. 'You know Shein? They're brilliant.'

'I do,' the doctor said chattily. 'I do indeed.'

And as I parked my backside on the chair, which was blue and plastic and uncomfortable, I thought, as the door closed, how very, very Sammy. The character we'd come to know was still in there.

I was about twenty minutes into my vigil in the waiting area when my mobile rang: Christine. And with another person now in the seat next to me, clearly deep into an absorbing paperback, I decided to stretch my legs and take a walk outside to talk.

'You've just saved my bottom from going into cramp,' I told her, chuckling. 'I'm at the hospital with Sammy,' I clarified. 'He's in with the psychiatrist. She seems very nice. I –'

'Good,' she said briskly. 'Look, I have some news I need to share with you.'

I could tell from her tone that this wasn't about ashes or personal effects. Oh dear Lord, what on earth was she about to tell me?

'Sounds a bit ominous,' I said, pushing open the door I had finally found that led outside. 'What's wrong?'

'Some good news first,' Christine said. 'They found Kenny. He's been arrested and is currently in custody on remand.'

'Oh, thank God for that,' I said. 'Has he admitted everything? Do they know exactly what he was up to?'

'More than any of us envisaged,' she said flatly. 'I'm afraid he was part of a much larger organisation. A network of paedophiles that all had access to thousands of images of children – including Sammy, of course, in various states of undress and … well, I'm sure you can imagine it for yourself. But the scary part is that as well as these images being shared and sold, details of a number of the children were shared too, including their phone numbers, addresses and other personal information.'

'What?' I squeaked. '*Really*?'

'Really. It's just horrendous.'

I let that sink in, feeling shocked – though I wasn't really sure why I should be, because everyone knew this sort of thing happened, after all. Why else did children have it constantly drummed into them that they should never talk to strangers, or accept sweeties, or get in people's cars? But just the thought of them being watched, being targeted, being followed …

'So, they've all been arrested too, then?' I asked hopefully.

'No, they haven't,' Christine said. 'Though lots of information about the ring has been found on Kenny's computer, rounding them all up is proving to be difficult. And might not even happen – as you can imagine, there will be all kinds of false identities in the mix and I don't doubt a lot will have covered their tracks. You know how these things work, what with the dark web and everything. You can never *really* be sure, can you?' She paused. 'Which is why I also have bad news.'

'That's not bad news enough?'

She sighed. 'No. Because the bottom line is that we have to move Sammy.'

Of course. That had been the reason for Christine's tone and trepidation. They obviously had to move him for his own safety. But *did* they have to? Could they be absolutely sure these characters knew where he lived?

'Oh, bloody hell, Christine, do they *have* to? I mean, is he really at risk? He's with us, after all, and he can obviously change his mobile number. I was already thinking that maybe the best thing is that we get a new phone – fresh start and all that, and we can also –'

'We have to move him,' she repeated. 'We have a duty of care and we would be failing in that duty if we left him vulnerable to these criminal gangs. I know it's the last thing you want to hear, but his safety is paramount and –'

'But this'll really knock him back,' I said. '*Really* knock him back. And just when he's beginning to get his head around everything and is feeling more positive about the future – and so much of *that's* because he trusts us – because he thinks he's staying *with* us. We've *promised* him …'

I tailed off, too upset to go on. Yes, Sammy might be safer, but his mental health would take such a huge nosedive …

'I know,' Christine said. 'And I'm as gutted as you are. But we have no choice. And it *will* be the best thing in the long run – we both know that. A new home, far away, where nobody can find him. A proper fresh start, where he will have a chance to thrive.'

But would he? Would he not just be plunged back into loneliness and depression, his trust once again shattered? How on earth was I going to spin this to make it better for him?

It was such a lovely day, the sun warm on my back. But my mood could not have been blacker. I felt so upset. Not with Christine – she was just doing her job – but at the prospect of losing Sammy, of telling him that, despite all my promises, he was to be shipped off to live with strangers yet again. But mostly I was angry. Angry that a group of disgusting people could destroy so many young lives and, even when exposed, could still have such far-reaching and long-lasting effects on their victims.

'I understand that,' I told Christine, since I had no choice but to do so. 'Though it doesn't make it any easier. So, when? What's the plan? Has a new family been found yet?'

'Not as yet,' she said. 'We're liaising with a local authority, who say they have a couple of options. I'll obviously keep you in the loop though. I'm hoping to have more news tomorrow. But, ballpark, I imagine we're talking around a fortnight, so you'll need to start preparing him – as best you can, anyway. I'd suggest Jen coming round to break the news to him, but she's still off work, and, to be honest with you, I think it's best coming from you anyway, don't you?'

'Of course,' I said, grim as the task was going to be.

'I'm *genuinely* really sorry,' Christine added. Though she really didn't need to. Like all of us, I knew she was just doing what was best for Sammy.

Would he see it like that though? I didn't think so.

Chapter 21

I was dreading Sammy coming out of Dr Summers' office. He had gone in so upbeat and positive, and now I had this bombshell to drop on him. And with just two weeks, give or take, till he was going to be shipped off again, I couldn't put off telling him for very long. But I would at least wait a day, till I'd spoken to Mike and we had time to give some thought as to how we were going to frame it for Sammy so that it didn't feel quite as wretched as it was.

There was also the small matter that he had just spent an hour with a psychiatrist, and if there was one thing I definitely knew about such encounters it was that all kinds of emotional storms might be set off.

So, right now, at least, my priority was that. One thing at a time seemed to be the way to go.

I painted on my biggest smile as I watched him come out of the office. The boy who refused to engage clearly now had; Sammy was light on his feet, shoulders down and grinning from ear to ear.

'You all done then?' I asked, standing up to greet him. 'You seem happy.'

'It's all good,' he said. 'I'm going to be seeing Leah – sorry, I mean Dr Summers – every week now for a while. She's got a really cool office. There are bean bags instead of chairs and it's even got a hot chocolate machine!'

'Hot chocolate, in this weather?' I said, rubbing his arm and trying not to focus on that 'every week now for a while' bit.

'Leah is fine,' the doctor said, from behind him. She tapped the side of her nose. 'And the chocolate machine doesn't come out for just anybody, you know, so we'll keep that between us, okay?'

I thanked her and made a mental note that I – we – *someone* – would have to let the hospital know that the meetings would be stopping sooner rather than later. Another frustration I could do nothing about. Yet again, Sammy would have to meet and learn to trust a new professional. I just hoped it would be somebody he clicked with as much as he clearly had with this one. Despite my having already made clear to him that he didn't have to discuss anything he'd talked to Dr Summers about, since that was obviously confidential, as soon as we set off for the hospital car park, he seemed keen to fill me in.

'She spoke about coercion and manipulation and things,' he said, 'the same stuff you all did, and asked me a bit of stuff about how it made me feel when I ran away and went into Kenny's house, and about all the things I'm working out in my head now, you know? She said it was good that I'm thinking about, you know, the things he'd done and so on, and that I'm thinking about why I went along with it all. She said it's like it gave me something I needed, you know, to feel he was looking out for me and asked about my nana and that, and what it was like for me when she died. She thinks it's all about security,' he added, the torrent of words slowing down now, '– like, a feeling of being wanted, because of Nana dying, and my mum never having been there and that.'

We'd reached the car now and he smiled over the roof at me as he waited for me to unlock it.

'She's cool. I really get her, you know?'

'It sounds like you do, sweetheart,' I said, as we both opened our doors. 'I'm so happy that you've found it helpful. Sometimes it's good to talk to someone who's completely outside of a situation, isn't it? Onwards and upwards. Let's hope things keep getting better, eh?'

'They will,' Sammy said, once we'd both climbed into the car. And he really sounded like he meant it, which made me feel even gloomier. 'Oh, and you know those photos you took of my nan's tree? Can we choose a couple to print off, so I can start painting it when we get home? Only Leah said it would be a really good thing for me to do – sort of like homework – because she says it will help unlock some nice memories and stuff, so I thought I could give that a go this afternoon? By the way, when am I back in school? I'm kind of getting bored being stuck at home now – no offence or anything, obvs, but am I going back next week?'

Much as I was glad that he'd finally asked about the photographs, at the same time knowing what I knew now was like being stabbed with lots of tiny pins. I hated having to lie to him. Perhaps Mike and I should tell him this evening after all.

'Yes, I think that's a great idea,' I said, since there was no choice but to soldier on. 'I bet it *will* bring back some lovely memories. As for school though, not just yet. They want to wait till you're properly better, properly rested – and I agree with them. You've been through a lot, love, after all.'

He seemed to take this on the chin. 'Oh, okay, I suppose. Actually, Leah said something like that too. Said I needed rest for my mind too, not just my body.'

'Exactly,' I said, feeling gloomier still. It was good to hear he was beginning to accept that he'd been abused. But as for that mental rest – how? Because we were now just going to add to his emotional turmoil.

As planned, after we'd printed off a few images of Sammy's tree, he went up to his bedroom and spent the rest of the day painting. I'd been firm on my 'no messy paints in the bedroom' rule thus far, but in this case he didn't want me to see it till he was finished, and figuring we were in a different place than we had been a few weeks back, I waived it and helped him take his easel and paints and assorted paraphernalia upstairs.

I was still unsure whether to speak to him that night or in the morning, torn between getting an unpleasant task out of the way and letting him enjoy another peaceful night of sleep first. So, I distracted myself by doing an online grocery shop then, having also done an inventory of what needed using up to clear space in the fridge and freezer, cooked up a big pan of Bolognaise sauce and made the sauce for Sammy's favourite chicken curry.

Sammy was still upstairs painting when Mike got in from work and when I told him tea was almost ready, he said he was still deep 'in the zone' and asked if it was okay if he had his food later. Which suited me fine, and since Mike was happy to eat later, it gave us time to have a chat about Christine's depressing news and my plan to break the news to Sammy the following morning.

Mike was, naturally, as shocked and saddened as I was about it all and questioned the need for him to be whisked away quite so soon: 'I mean, the lad's got no smartphone and we can keep him safe, can't we? Couldn't there at least be a hiatus while he gets himself together?'

I'd been thinking exactly that while I'd been cooking. We could surely make a case for delaying things, couldn't we? But then I'd changed my mind: 'I thought the same at first,' I said to Mike, 'but when you think about it, it'll probably make things worse. Christine was clear: he's being relocated far, far away and that'll be the end of it so to keep him here for any length of time would probably make the leaving more traumatic when we got to it, because he'd be all settled, so it would come as such a shock to him, wouldn't it? And if we were to tell him he's moving on down the line, then why delay? Plus, maybe it's better to have that clear connection between what's been done to him by those monsters and the need to start afresh somewhere else?'

'I take your point, I suppose,' Mike said. 'But two weeks? It seems a very short time for the lad to get his head around yet another move. But it is what it is,' he added, shaking his head. 'You sure you wouldn't rather tell him tonight, while I'm home?'

I told him that I'd decided I'd rather allow Sammy a good night's sleep. 'So tonight,' I said, 'we'll just be a normal family – as normal as our family ever is, that is – and keep the new peaceful mood for at least another evening.'

'You're the boss,' Mike said.

So, once Sammy called down to ask us to come up and see what he'd created, we duly reaffixed our 'normal' faces and headed up the stairs.

The room smelled pleasingly of paint. And though the painting itself was still wet – and being oil paint, it would be for some time yet – he'd carefully draped a sheet over the easel so we couldn't see it right away. 'Now,' he said, 'when you look at this, you have to bear in mind that Doctor Leah told me to let my imagination run wild, okay?'

Then, by way of further clarification, he added, 'I told her I liked people like Vincent van Gogh and she said she did too. And did you know? He had, like, a shedload of mental health problems, and even had to go to a hospital for a while, and did you know he was so unhappy that one day he even cut off his own *ear*?! But he also made paintings that were, like, well, *proper* crazy. All swirls and whirls, and twirly bits, and loads of mad colours. He just, basically, like, *went* for it. So that's what I tried to do – to just go for it. So, it might not look exactly like a tree, or my nan's garden, or anything, but that's what you have to keep in mind – that it's an *impression*. Which is where the word *impressionists* comes from,' he added, 'like Monet and so on.'

Listening to Sammy's brief introduction to this latest work, which obviously meant so much to him, it occurred to me that he probably already knew more about fine art than I ever would. Another pinprick of regret. He'd be saying goodbye to that supportive art teacher as well.

'Anyway,' he finished, holding a corner of the sheet, 'you both ready?'

'More than,' Mike said. 'So, come on, then. The suspense is killing us!'

'Tah-dah!' Sammy said as he lifted the sheet carefully to reveal what was, undeniably, a beautiful painting.

'Oh my goodness!' I said, stepping forward to get a better, close-up look, 'no wonder it's taken you all afternoon, Sammy. This is, well … it's amazing!'

'That's flippin' brilliant, that is, son,' Mike agreed. 'I didn't realise we had our own little Van Gogh living with us, Case!'

A Family Friend

Sammy beamed. 'Do you really like it?'

'Listen, lad,' Mike said. 'Case and I don't know much about art – well, except that we know what we like and what we don't like, I suppose, and that's fine for us. And this we *very* much like. I can't believe that you did all this in the space of a few hours.'

But I kind of could. Sammy had natural talent, clearly – that had been obvious from the start – but what he also had was a complete lack of fear when he painted. I'd seen it myself. When he painted, he just played, he just let his instinct guide him. Because he did it for himself, for pleasure, and (obviously) for therapy, he had no agenda. Like he'd said, he just went for it, and though that had ended up with the creation of some very disturbing images along the way, the doing of them obviously had had value – in him expressing himself to us without having to use words, as the PIPA therapist had pointed out. And it also showed here: he hadn't just painted what he'd seen, he also created a feeling. Yes, I could see a tree, and a vaguely garden-like landscape, but it was much more about capturing nature doing nature – the white swirls of petals, the sinuous shapes of trunk and branches, the whole set in a riotous, multi-coloured sky – and if it didn't exactly resemble that bland, suburban terrace where its real counterpart stood, who even cared? It was evoking a feeling. And, in me, an emotion. And that emotion was happiness. That he had captured the tree that he'd wanted to capture; the one he and his nan had both planted and nurtured.

'It's absolutely stunning,' I told him, truthfully. 'Your nan would be *so* pleased and proud.'

'*I'm* proud,' he said. Then added, 'And now I'm *starving*. Is that curry I can smell?'

'It is indeed,' I said.

Perhaps one of the last I'd ever cook for him. *Damn that evil man to hell*, I thought, as we all trooped back down the stairs.

Delivering difficult or distressing news is never easy, particularly when it comes to children. It's even harder when the child is already disadvantaged or unhappy, and you know that you're about to make them feel even worse. Yes, it's part of the job, of course, but it never gets any easier, so if there's any chance of doing it with that proverbial spoonful of sugar, that's obviously going to be a help.

Having tossed and turned a fair bit in the night, I had come round to the understanding that what was happening was definitely in Sammy's best interests. To get him right away from his 'uncle' wasn't just about how things stood now, it was also about the future. I knew both from personal experience and from countless stories I'd heard down the years that, particularly with the connectedness that came with the many forms of social media, there might come a time, a few months hence, or even a few years hence, when Sammy, in common with many previously groomed and abused children, might re-establish contact with the man he'd for so long thought of as his family. He might look him up, say, just out of curiosity. Or might, because they often did, change the narrative in his mind; see what happened to him at the man's hand through rose-tinted glasses. Or, once out of prison – and that day would surely come – Kenny might want to find *him*. So, yes, it was right that Sammy was physically far away. That distance between them would give him far greater safety.

But for Sammy, here and now, it would obviously be a blow and was a job I definitely wasn't looking forward to, so any spoonfuls of sugar that could potentially wing my way would be fallen on very gratefully. Not that I anticipated that happening any time soon. Indeed, when I saw that I had a text from Christine at around seven the following morning, my first thought was obviously, *oh dear, what now?*

But when I opened it, I was to be pleasantly surprised: *I have a little bit of good news for you, it read. Call when you can.*

Having just poured my third coffee of the morning, I called her immediately.

'Are you at work already?' I asked. 'I know Mike goes into work at silly o-clock, but don't tell me you are too, now. The world's going mad!'

Christine laughed. 'No, not yet. I'm heading in, in half an hour or so. I just thought I'd text as I've been skimming though my emails and I've had one from the funeral directors who dealt with Sammy's nan's funeral. Well, I say funeral. As we thought might be the case, she didn't actually have one. Had one of those direct cremations lots of people are opting for these days.'

I knew about those because my sister's partner's late mother had opted for one. She wasn't religious and she also had a deep and abiding hatred of crematoriums – hated the whole business of the curtains shutting, and the chimney, and the ominous curls of smoke, so had made it clear that she didn't want anyone having to attend one on her account and had left money for a big wake at her local pub instead. Had that been the case here, I wondered?

'I'm not sure,' Christine said, 'I haven't actually spoken to the contact there. I just emailed and it turns out that they still have her ashes. Apparently, if no one claims them, they have to keep them for five years before disposing of them. Lucky or what? Another year or so and they'd have been lost to us.'

'That is *such* good news,' I said, feeling a welcome sense of relief. Though I couldn't change the bad news I was going to have to share with Sammy, this was really going to help. 'I can't tell you what a difference that's going to make. Can we go and collect them?'

'Yes, of course. Well, someone can, anyway. I'll have to call them once their office opens to find out the details. I imagine that normally, as her next of kin, her daughter would be the one to have them, but since she obviously didn't make arrangements to collect them, and is no longer in contact, she's waived her right to have them now. Such an odd situation, isn't it? So sad.'

'Tell me about it. Every part of that poor kid's start in life has been so sad. But it is what it is, I guess. And this will mean *so* much to Sammy. And what about her personal effects? Did you manage to find out anything about that?'

'Not as yet, but I'll ask when I call them, I promise. Oh, and before I forget, you have the go-ahead to get him a new phone. Just a dumb phone, of course – a basic supermarket one. But at least it'll mean he can keep in touch till he gets his own one back. In fact, we'll probably be able to allow him a new smartphone once he's settled with his new family – to be used under supervision of course, at least for the time being. But that should also give him a sense that he's getting his life back on track.'

'And I can tell him that? You know, now – I'm going to break the news once he's woken up.'

Christine thought for a moment 'Yes,' she said. 'I don't see why not. Anyway, I'd better get my skates on. I'll report back once I have any further news, probably later on this morning. In the meantime, good luck. I hope the poor lad doesn't take it too badly.'

Though I couldn't imagine Sammy taking what I had no choice but to impart to him anything other than badly, the news about his nan's ashes really was a piece of very welcome good luck. I had no idea what he would want to do with them – perhaps he'd like to sprinkle the majority somewhere and keep a few grains inside a piece of jewellery – but just that sense of having something of her to keep close to him would mean the world, I was sure. When he finally ambled downstairs a couple of hours later, I decided there was no point in delaying the inevitable – indeed, I didn't want to. I wanted him to know exactly where he stood, so we could concentrate on the business of getting him a new phone and, hopefully, going to collect his nan's ashes.

'Morning, sweetie,' I said, as he slid his bottom up onto a bar stool, 'You want a coffee? Only before we sort your breakfast, we need to sit and have a talk.'

His face fell immediately. 'Oh, God,' he said. 'What have I done?'

'Absolutely nothing,' I reassured him as I slipped a mug under the coffee machine and went to get the oat milk from the fridge. 'It's about what's going to happen in a couple of weeks or so.' I stopped and looked directly at him. 'It's not going to be what you want to hear, I don't think. It wasn't what I wanted to hear either. But it's what's got to happen, I'm afraid. You're going to be moved on to another family. For your safety –'

'My safety? I'm safe here, aren't I?'

'*Yes,*' I said. 'As far as Mike and I are concerned, *yes*. But it's not up to us, and hard as it has been for me to get my head around it, I *do* think it's the right thing for you.'

Sammy gawped at me. 'Why? *Why* is it the right thing for me?' his eyes narrowed. 'Or is it just the right thing for *you*?'

A Family Friend

'Oh, love,' I said, as the coffee machine hissed and burbled behind me. 'You *know* that's not true. Or at least I *hope* by now you do. This is all about your safety and wellbeing, Sammy. And the situation we're in currently.'

'What situation?'

'The situation with your Uncle Kenny.' I poured milk into the coffee and passed it across to him. 'He's been arrested now –'

He wrapped his hand around the mug. 'So what's the problem then? Why am I not safe?'

'Because it's not just about Kenny, it's about all the other men he was associating with. It's about keeping you safe from *them*.'

Because honesty was unquestionably the right policy in this kind of situation, I did not hold back. I told Sammy pretty much everything that Christine had told me. About the web of people who made their living trading in child pornography – who not only distributed images and videos of the kind Sammy knew only too well about, but who also sought out and groomed children both by using multiple aliases on social media and who were also responsible for creating all that online content – a business that was far from online and very much IRL. Real children, being groomed and exploited and abused. Real kids whose In Real Life details some of them knew. I harked back to the conversations he'd had with my grandson. None of this was news to him, was it? After all, he was the one who had warned Levi about it.

Sammy had been sipping his coffee as I spoke. Now he placed the mug down and lifted his gaze to me.

'So, they think they'll come after me, is that it?' he asked. 'You know, for getting Kenny arrested? And other ones too?'

'No, I don't think that, actually,' I told him, because I genuinely didn't. 'I think many of those who've not been caught will have gone to ground now.'

And hopefully never show their sick faces again, I thought. But they would; they would pop up again somewhere. Because those people always did.

'But as your legal guardians, social services cannot possibly take that risk. If they know where you live, where you go to school, who you hang out with and so on … Well, they would be failing in their duty of care to you if they didn't try to keep you out of harm's way, wouldn't they? Which means moving you to another part of the country where you can have a whole new start. Where –'

'Where? Where are they sending me?'

'I don't know, love. Not yet. But we should hear very soon.'

'But what if I hate them? And what about you and Mike? Will I ever see you again? What about school, my friends, my new doctor? Is that it? That all just ends, just like that?'

'Sammy,' I said, 'there's nothing I'd love more than for you to be able to stay here with us, for you to go back to your school and continue with Dr Summers, I promise you that. I *swear*. And I also promise that we always want you to be in our lives. We can phone each other, FaceTime and Snapchat – well, if you show me how to do it – and me and Mike, we –'

'But I don't even have a fucking *phone*!'

There were tears shining in his eyes now, as everything began to sink in. What a wretched job it was to have to tell a child something like this.

I went around the breakfast bar and put my arms around him. 'You will, love. I've been told we can go and pick up a new one for you. Only a Nokia, a basic one,' I hastened to add before he got his hopes up. 'But that's just for now. Once you're in your new place, you'll be able to have another smartphone, to use till yours is returned to you, and –'

'A bloody Nokia?!' He was crying hard now – and why wouldn't he be? And I was struggling not to cry myself.

'But, love,' I whispered, 'I do have a tiny bit of good news as well. Your nan's ashes? We've located them. It looks like we can go and collect them. The funeral directors have –'

He wriggled away from me, forcibly, and dragged the heels of his hands across his eyes.

'My nan's ashes? My whole fucking life has been fucked over, *again*! And you think a pile of old ashes is going to *change* anything?'

Then, sending his coffee mug skittering across the worktop, he whirled around and ran from the room.

I caught the mug before it pitched straight over the edge.

Well, I thought miserably, *what the hell else did I expect?*

Chapter 22

They say all political careers end in failure, don't they? Because that's the nature of politics and human affairs. In fostering, we like to think that most placements will have happier outcomes. That the child will ultimately end up in a better place than the one they were in when they came to you – it's that optimism, that faith, that keeps driving you forwards, even though most of us who've been doing this job for any length of time know that sometimes that's not how it goes.

With Sammy, however, I did keep that faith. Hard as the move was going to be for him, I understood why it had to happen and trusted that his life chances could, and would, be better if he could only make a fresh start somewhere else. So, Christine's next call, when it came in, was a blessing.

After Sammy had thundered back up the stairs to his bedroom, I'd left it a few minutes before following him up there, but could no more leave him to stew in it than fly. And though his initial reaction had been to yell at me to go away, after a time he'd calmed down enough to let me go in and sit and stroke his back while, curled under his duvet, he cried. But you can't cry forever, and, after a time, the tears stopped, and though I knew it would take a while before he could properly process this new development, I felt happy enough to leave him to shower and dress while I went back down to make us both some food.

I was putting a pizza in the oven – Sammy's choice – when my phone rang.

'So, here's the lowdown,' Christine said, once we'd quickly debriefed about how things had gone with 'the talk'. 'I'll pop it all in an email when I get a moment later, but since I've got the address of the funeral directors for you anyway, I thought I'd could run it all by you now. We've got a family. Very experienced. Couple called Jane and Chris Mawson, grown-up children flown the nest, and I have to say they sound like a really good match.'

She went on to tell me all about the family they had found, who lived in a small town by the coast, about two hundred miles away. They'd fostered lots of children, some of whom had been among the most damaged in the system, and were currently looking after a fourteen-year-old girl, who'd apparently been with them since the age of seven after her father died from a drug overdose and then, nine months later, her mother had committed suicide. Really, really sad, but over the worst of it all now, thank goodness.

'And she's a really girly girl,' Christine said, obviously reading from notes she'd been given. 'Into all things pink and glittery – so hopefully right up Sammy's street – and who is well settled and will be staying with them into adulthood. Oh, and it says here, she's a real fashionista! They also have two dogs, both Chihuahuas, called Pippa and Penny, and it says here that they like going out for family meals, are quite outdoorsy and love going to the cinema. Oh, and bowling – how about that? A match made in heaven, eh? Oh, and the girl, who's called Skye, is apparently very excited. Their own children are in their late twenties, so the girl's essentially an only child and has been hoping for a sibling for a long time. They feel Sammy would be a great choice, and so do we.'

I agreed that they did indeed sound perfect for Sammy. Though whether *he* felt like that we, of course, couldn't know. And wouldn't, till he'd actually moved in there. But the boy who moved in there would be a very different person to the one who'd been living that damaging other life, his strings pulled by a network of despicable people and exhibiting multiple signs of deep distress. But he was better now. A way to go still, but, despite the traumas of the last few distressing days, all the signs were moving in the right direction. So, yes, I had faith that there was now every chance that the brighter future we all wanted for him would be his for the taking.

'So, do we have a potential date?'

'Yes, the Saturday after next. We thought a weekend, obviously.'

'And we're to take him?' I asked. 'Given Jen's still off work?'

'We've discussed that – it's way too far.'

'We wouldn't mind, it's –'

'Absolutely not. We really couldn't ask that of you. So we're hoping for James – just got to check his availability.'

'What, outreach worker James? That would be highly unusual.'

'Trainee social worker James now,' Christine corrected me.

'Oh, that's wonderful!' I said. 'He seemed such a natural.'

And if he *was* free, I thought, also the ideal person to take Sammy. Christine was right, it would be a slog for us to make such a lengthy round trip. And was probably better anyway – my instinct was that James would be an ideal road-trip companion. And it would make for less angst and stress all round, even if they were squidged in his little Mini. 'And the funeral directors?'

'I'll text the details across to you now. You can visit anytime, basically, during their usual opening hours. Just call first to let them know when you're coming. Oh, and you're authorised to pay for a scattering tube too,' she added. 'There are a few choices of design on their website – I thought Sammy could choose.'

A Family Friend

Assuming Sammy even cared, I thought, once I'd rung off. But again, I kept the faith. Once he got his head around it, I was certain he would.

And there was no time like the present.

Setting the timer for the pizza, I headed back upstairs. Later tonight, once the email about the Mawsons had come, I would write one of my own so they could learn a little more about Sammy and have time to get stocked up on oat milk. I would also call the family – Christine had encouraged me to do so – and perhaps try to organise a Teams meeting too. But, for Sammy himself, news of the family could wait. Only when he expressed any interest in knowing more, which I doubted would be yet, would I sit down with him and pass on all their details. More important, to my mind, was that sprinkling tube of ashes.

Sammy was out of the bathroom and back in his bedroom, and dressed now in T-shirt and joggers. He was wielding a paintbrush and adding a few details to the painting that had brought us all such joy the previous night.

I walked in and sat down on the bed. 'How are you doing, love?' I asked him. 'Or is that a silly question?'

Sammy shrugged his skinny shoulders. 'I'm resigned, I guess,' he said. 'Not a lot I can do about it, is there?'

I wasn't sure if his flat, accepting tone was worse than the tears earlier, but there was nothing I could do about that so it was pointless to keep offering up platitudes. But there was still one thing I could do: 'You know, love, you can take all my dad's art stuff with you. It's been such a joy to see it all being used.'

'That's very kind,' he said, placing the brush he'd been using back in its pot of cleaner. 'Thank you.'

But his polite tone that made me wince, hammering home, as it did, how he must now feel that distance between us. That knowledge that we would very soon no longer be his carers. But it prompted me to act – to stand up and go across to him and put my arm around his shoulders.

'Can I take payment in hugs?' I asked. 'I'm going to really miss our hugs.'

He turned towards me now and allowed me to properly embrace him. 'I'm just so *sad*,' he said, holding tight to me.

'Of course you are, love. So am I. I'm going to cry buckets when you go, believe me. But you must never, ever feel that Mike and I won't be there for you – you've seen our snug. Every face you see in there, every child – they *all* know that. And lots of them – some who are now in their twenties – still keep in touch.'

I felt him chuckle then. Less a sound than a rumble against my chest. 'And when I'm gone, you'll stick my photo up and when people come round you can say, "Ah, that's Sammy. The one who destroyed our coffee table."'

'I can and I will,' I said, pulling back and grinning. 'And, strictly between you and me, you did us a *big* favour. Anyway, that pizza should be ready, so we need to crack on. We've errands to go and run this afternoon.'

Sammy made a big show of frowning. 'To go get me a Nokia? Yee flippin' hah!'

'Yeehah indeed,' I said. 'You have yet to discover the joy of playing Snake.'

'Snake?'

'You'll see. Plus, we have another thing to sort out for you, don't we?'

'What?'

'Your nan's ashes.'

He looked shocked. 'You mean we're *actually* going to *do* that?'

'We are absolutely going to do that.' I had to remember he was only thirteen. What experience would he have had of such matters?

'But what am I supposed to do with them?' he asked, as he followed me down the stairs.

'Scatter them somewhere. Somewhere that was special to your nan? Or, if you can't think right now, maybe keep them for a bit? And, you know,' I added, as we entered the back room and I reached for a tea towel so I could get the pizza out, 'what a lot of people do is keep a few grains and have them put in a little container, like your friend at school, or in a locket. Something to think about anyway.'

He pulled a decidedly thirteen-year-old face, then smiled his lovely smile. 'C'mon, Casey,' he said. 'Isn't that, like, a bit *gross*?'

And in that instant, the distance between us disappeared. We would always stay in touch, I just knew it in my bones. And something else too: that Sammy was going to be okay.

Chapter 23

Leaving days never get any easier. You'd think after all these years, I would have grown a stronger backbone, but when the day came around I woke up with the same sinking feeling I always had, and probably always would, which I knew wouldn't leave me till the parting finally happened and it morphed into the inevitable tears. Though as I took the coffee Mike was holding out, having just packed some sandwiches and snacks and drinks for Sammy and James' journey, it was at least in the knowledge that Sammy was going to a wonderful new home and that he had every chance of a bright and happy future.

Having been on the funeral director's website, and after a confirmatory phone call, we'd gone and collected the cremated remains of Sammy's nan the previous Friday. There having been no magnolia trees on offer, he'd chosen a scattering tube with a wraparound photo of a bluebell wood.

'But it's still all a bit gross,' he declared once we were back in my car and he was sitting in the passenger seat with the tube between his legs. 'I mean – "cremated remains" – couldn't they think of something less icky? Feels, like, *so* weird to think that my nan is in here. I won't lie – to be honest, it's creeping me out a bit. I mean, it's nice and that, I s'pose. I reckon *she'd* be pleased, wouldn't she? After spending so long sitting on a shelf in that place. God, what must it be like to have that as your job? Must be a very, *very* weird place to work.'

'*Very* weird,' I agreed. And I couldn't help but smile. Ah, the pragmatism of children! But I guessed this was more about the passage of time than anything. Sammy had had years now to come to terms with his loss and perhaps my determination to give him some closure said more about my fifty-something sensibilities than his own emotional needs. Still, creeped out or not by having his nan travelling with us, I knew that, at least at some point, Sammy would be glad that we'd done this.

Were doing this, though only after a little bit of high-speed 'death admin', to use another rather icky phrase. Having given the matter some thought, Sammy had decided he didn't want to keep his nan's ashes. He instead wanted to put her at rest somewhere meaningful for her, but not, to my great relief, beneath the magnolia tree they had won at the school fete and planted outside her house – I could only imagine the awkward conversation I'd have had to have with the current tenants, had that been the case. They might feel pretty creeped out as well. But no, he didn't want to revisit that road, or any of the memories associated with Kenny, he wanted her to go beneath another magnolia – a big one in the park that was close to where they'd lived, and where he'd spent time sitting on a bench when he'd run away.

I'd been fearful at first, because I was anxious about going back there at all, to be honest – how would he fare going back to the scene of such distress? Would it not, to use the modern parlance, be 'triggering'? So, I'd asked if he was sure and he had been quick to reassure me. None of that mattered. It would be a return to a happy time in his life when his nan would take him to the park and where, in the summer, they'd have picnics together.

'Always with Scotch eggs,' he said. 'My nan was *mad* for Scotch eggs. And she'd always take a little pot of salt around with her, so she could sprinkle it on the egg bit. Isn't it funny the things you remember?'

So, after a flurry of emails to someone at the council, I'd managed to get the all-important permission: we were allowed to scatter the ashes there as long as we adhered to the rules. To be aware of any wind, to take care where we scattered and to be discreet – to be mindful of other park-users' feelings and privacy.

Ashes duly collected, once we were headed there, I was confident we could do so. There was no wind and sufficient late spring rain was falling to make it likely that the park would be mostly empty.

I was right. Having easily found a space in the all-but-empty car park, we flipped up hoods and made our way to a small, partly wooded but still manicured area, where the tree in question clearly had taken rightful pride of place. It was still in bloom, just, but many petals had now fallen, making a pretty pink carpet that circled the trunk.

'So, what do I do?' Sammy asked, once we'd arrived at the spot. 'Do I just, like, tip it out, or do I spread it around?'

'I don't think there are any rules, really,' I told him. 'You might want to walk around the tree a couple of times, sprinkling as you go and, you know, thinking about your nan, maybe talking to her as you walk round? You could even recite a poem perhaps ...'

I stopped. He was giving me what my mum would call an 'old-fashioned look', as if to say, did I really want him to look like a complete wally? 'I know,' I said, as he pulled off the lid and passed it to me. 'Why don't you tell her all about your painting? Only in your head, of course. I don't want to intrude.'

He grinned. 'You're alright. God, this is just about the weirdest thing I have *ever* done.' Then he set off, and his commentary – clearly audible, since he obviously *did* want to include me – was totally priceless, beginning with, 'Well, Nan, here we go ... I can't believe I'm actually doing this. I'm under your favourite tree, by the way, and it is literally pissing down with rain – well, not literally, obviously, hahaha – and I'm here with Casey, who's my foster mum, and she's trying *so* hard not to laugh, because this is bonkers, and if you're up there, I'm sure you're gonna be proper belly-laughing …' And so on and so forth till he'd completed three circuits and the remains of his beloved nan were all scattered.

And I knew neither of us would ever forget it.

And here we were, a week later, and James was due in less than half an hour. And our few short months with Sammy were going to come to an end. And it was, well, as far as it could be, okay. I'd told him all about the new family he was going to, and them all about him, and they'd since had two FaceTimes, which had both gone really well. And they'd also confirmed that once he'd been there a couple of weeks, they were going to get him set up with a new smartphone.

In the meantime, as well as discovering the 'joys' of playing Snake, Sammy had added our phone numbers to his small list of contacts, including that of Levi, who, to my delight, had suggested himself that it would be cool if they kept in touch. Down the line, he suggested, once Sammy had the means to do so, they could even 'meet up' to do some gaming together.

We'd also packed up the bulk of the art stuff and I could only cross my fingers that it would all fit in James' car (given that Sammy's trainer collection alone would probably take up half the boot). All bar the most recent of Sammy's oil paintings, that is, them being obviously not yet dry enough to travel. So, we'd be custodians, I reassured him, till they were dry.

'How are you doing, lovely?' I said, as he trotted down the stairs for the last time with his last remaining bits. 'I've packed a bunch of supplies for the journey, but do you want a last coffee in a travel mug?'

Sammy shook his head. He was looking very much the cool cat about town in his favourite jeans and trainers, and his sunshine yellow scarf – not so different to how he'd looked when he'd first come to us. 'I'll only need a wee before we're halfway down the road,' he said. And our eyes met, and both of us smiled a knowing smile. What a long way he had come.

'Right. Shall we start getting things outside?' Mike suggested, correctly sensing that I was at my usual emotional tipping point. 'With all this lot to pack in,' he said, casting an eye over the pile of bags and boxes, 'loading up the car might take a good while.'

'Oh, it'll be *fine*,' Sammy reassured him as he opened the front door. 'A lot of it's squidgy anyway, and – oh! Look at that!'

It seemed James had arrived, but he wasn't climbing out of a Mini. He was emerging, with a good deal less awkward-looking manoeuvring of his lower limbs, from a somewhat battered-looking but very cool 4X4.

'Wow,' Sammy said appreciatively. 'That's like a proper jeep, isn't it?'

'New wheels?' Mike said, as James bounded down the path towards us.

'Oh no, far from new,' he said. 'As you can probably see. It's got about 80K on the clock, but it's a good runner. And I do a lot of off-road-type stuff.'

'But where's your Mini?' I asked.

'Oh,' he said, 'that's not mine, it's my sister's. She had twins a few months back and she really struggled to get them in it so we did a swap for a bit – till she could afford a bigger car.'

I laughed. 'Aha! Mystery solved, then.'

'Mystery?'

'Why anyone with legs as long as yours would want to drive around in such a tiny car! Congratulations, by the way, on your new job. And for taking Sammy, of course.'

'Roadddtrippp!' Sammy added, clearly pumped at the prospect. 'I can't wait! So, shall we start getting loaded up?'

Then he glanced at me, and grinned, and then rolled those big hazel eyes. 'You're not *crying* already, are you?' he teased, pulling me in for a cuddle.

'Buckets and buckets,' I told him. 'Just as I promised.'

But it was as nothing to the amount I was going to cry twenty minutes later when, having just about held it together while Mike and I waved Sammy and James off, I trudged morosely up to his bedroom.

It was the usual necessary task of stripping the bed, opening the windows and airing the room. Over the years, while Mike tended to potter downstairs, it had become, for me, something of a private ritual. I could of course put it off, let the dust settle a bit, but I actually found it cathartic; it was a moment to cry, to reflect, to dry my eyes and regroup, and, most importantly, to experience the moment of this often painful but integral part of the process.

The room was bright, and also tidy, and the windows were already open – the fresh, cool air helping to dry Sammy's recent artworks. And in pride of place, still on the easel, was his tree painting. Now, however, there was also a note perched on the sill.

I picked it up. It was a folded sheet of paper from one of his school – now former school – exercise books:

Dear Casey and Mike, the note read, *please accept this masterpiece (lol) in full and final payment for your (lovely) broken coffee table. I knew I wouldn't quite manage to say it without blubbing, but I wanted to thank you so much for all you've done for me. I honestly don't know where I'd be now if you hadn't done what you did. I'll never forget it and I'll never forget you either. I'm leaving you my favourite painting because I want you to always remember me. I know that each time you look at it, you'll think about that gorgeous kid you once had (hahaha …) xxxxxxxx*

And, of course, he was right. He had been, and we would.

Epilogue

Within a fortnight of Sammy leaving us, he sent us a letter which cheered us up no end. By the sound of things, he was having the time of his life and though I wasn't naive about the probable challenges ahead, it was heartening to hear how much fun he was having, particularly as the Mawsons apparently owned a motor-home and seemed to be spending their summer making very good use of it. And it certainly did sound idyllic.

Honestly, Casey, Sammy had written, *they don't even plan it! Jane just looks on her phone to see where is hot and sunny, and then we just pack up the dogs and set off! And Skye is super cool,* he'd also noted – again, much to my delight. *She's teaching me loads of TikTok dances and I'm allowed to share her iPad so long as we sit in the living room. Oh, I'm getting a new iPhone in September when I start my new school so I'll FaceTime you then!*

I couldn't have been happier to see all those exclamation marks, I can tell you.

* * *

On the other side of the coin, however, a couple of months after Sammy left us, Christine called to say 'Uncle' Kenny had tried to reach out. He'd apparently written a letter and had asked that it be sent to social services in the hope that it could be passed on to Sammy.

'He wanted to apologise for everything,' Christine told me. 'The whole thing is filled with remorse and an acknowledgement of the harm he's caused Sammy. I say "remorse" – I think I'd prefix that word with "apparent", because call me an old cynic but my feeling is that this is more about looking contrite to a judge and jury – what with his trial coming up – rather than an actual atonement for his heinous crimes.'

'Blimey, you're not going to share it with Sammy, are you?' I asked, appalled.

'Absolutely not,' she reassured me. 'We can see no benefit in doing so. And potentially a lot of emotional harm. No, the consensus is that it will simply be added to his file.'

'Good call!' I agreed, much relieved.

Three months after Sammy joined them, I'm pleased to be able to report that, as with Skye, the Mawsons asked that Sammy be allowed to stay with them till he reached independence and from our FaceTimes – which happened regularly as soon as he got his new iPhone – we could tell that it was a definitely a case of 'right time, right family'. Not our family this time, sadly, but that's sometimes how it goes. And as for his old phone and laptop, well, to be honest, since he never even asked about them, we were more than happy to hear that the normally efficient folk down at the local police hub had, er, unfortunately, um, mislaid them … Funny, that.

So, all in all, it really was a bright new beginning for Sammy. No reminders of that awful, awful past. But, for us, though I never did get round to pinching any magnolia seeds, there was one big, beautiful reminder of our time caring for him in the form of his magnificent impressionist tree painting, which we found a frame for and hung in the snug. And it was very much admired by my mum and dad when they next came for a visit. At least till Mum glanced around and spotted the absence of something she'd assumed she would also find in there.

'Where's our coffee table gone?' she huffed.

Oops!

CASEY WATSON

One woman determined to
make a difference.

Read Casey's poignant
memoirs and be inspired.

LITTLE GIRL LOST

Kelly suffers with bipolar disorder, and when she attempts to burn down the family home it becomes clear that her six-year-old daughter Amelie is in grave danger.

When she arrives at the home of foster carer Casey Watson, Amelie acts much younger than her age. Casey must get to the root of her behaviour, while doing what she can to keep the family together.

I WANT MY DADDY

Five-year-old Ethan is brought to Casey in the middle of the night after the sudden death of his young mother from a drug overdose

When arrangements are made for Ethan to see his dad in prison, Casey recognises the name and face . . . It turns out she's far more familiar with this case than first imagined.

I JUST WANT TO BE LOVED

Casey has fostered her share of vulnerable adolescents, but 14-year-old Elise brings unique challenges

When Elise makes some dark allegations against her mum, Casey doesn't know what to believe. Is Elise telling the truth? Casey is determined to find out and keep her safe.

MUMMY, PLEASE DON'T LEAVE

When baby Tommy – born in prison – and his half-brother, Seth, are placed in the Watsons' care, their troubled teenage mother soon follows suit

Can Casey find the energy and strength to see this unusual case through?

LET ME GO

Harley is an anxious teen
who wants to end her own life,
and there's only one woman
who can find out why

Casey makes a breakthrough which
sheds light on the disturbing truth –
there is a man in Harley's life, a
very dangerous man indeed.

A DARK SECRET

A troubled nine-year-old with
a violent streak, Sam's relentless
bullying sees even his siblings beg
not to be placed with him

When Casey delves into Sam's past
she uncovers something far darker
than she had imagined.

A BOY WITHOUT HOPE

A history of abuse and neglect
has left Miller destined for
life's scrap heap

Miller's destructive behaviour will push
Casey to her limits, but she is determined
to help him overcome his demons
and give him hope.

NOWHERE TO GO

Eleven-year-old Tyler has stabbed his stepmother and has nowhere to go

With his birth mother dead and a father who doesn't want him, what can be done to stop his young life spiralling out of control?

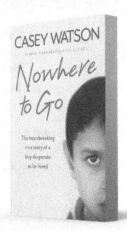

GROOMED

Keeley is urgently rehomed with Casey after accusing her foster father of abuse

It's Casey's job to keep Keeley safe, but can she protect this strong-willed teen from the dangers online?

THE SILENT WITNESS

Bella's father is on a ventilator, fighting for his life, while her mother is currently on remand in prison, charged with his attempted murder

Bella is the only witness.

RUNAWAY GIRL

Adrianna arrives on Casey's doorstep with no possessions, no English and no explanation

It will be a few weeks before Casey starts getting the shocking answers to her questions . . .

MUMMY'S LITTLE SOLDIER

Leo isn't a bad lad, but his frequent absences from school mean he's on the brink of permanent exclusion

Leo is clearly hiding something, and Casey knows that if he is to have any kind of future, it's up to her to find out the truth.

SKIN DEEP

Flip is being raised by her alcoholic mother, and comes to Casey after a fire at their home

Flip has Foetal Alcohol Syndrome (FAS), but it soon turns out that this is just the tip of the iceberg . . .

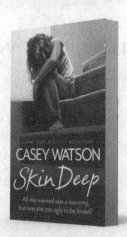

A STOLEN CHILDHOOD

Kiara appears tired and distressed, and the school wants Casey to take her under her wing for a while

On the surface, everything points to a child who is upset that her parents have separated. The horrific truth, however, shocks Casey to the core.

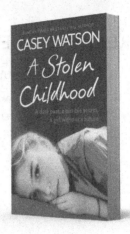

THE GIRL WITHOUT A VOICE

What is the secret behind Imogen's silence?

Discover the shocking and devastating past of a child with severe behavioural problems.

A LAST KISS FOR MUMMY

A teenage mother and baby in need of a loving home

At 14 Emma is just a child herself – and one who's never been properly mothered.

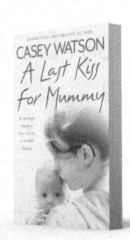

BREAKING THE SILENCE

Two boys with an unlikely bond

With Georgie and Jenson, Casey is
facing her toughest test yet.

MUMMY'S LITTLE HELPER

A young girl secretly caring
for her mother

Abigail has been dealing with
pressures no child should face. Casey
has the difficult challenge of helping
her to learn to let go.

TOO HURT TO STAY

Branded 'vicious and evil',
eight-year-old Spencer asks to
be taken into care

Casey and her family are disgusted: kids
aren't born evil. Despite the challenges
Spencer brings, they are determined to
help him find a loving home.

LITTLE PRISONERS

Abused siblings who do not know
what it means to be loved

With new-found security and trust,
Casey helps Ashton and Olivia to
rebuild their lives.

CRYING FOR HELP

A damaged girl haunted
by her past

Sophia pushes Casey to the limits,
threatening the safety of the whole
family. Can Casey make a
difference in time?

THE BOY NO ONE
LOVED

Five-year-old Justin was
desperate and helpless

Six years after being taken into care,
Justin has had 20 failed placements. Casey
and her family are his last hope.

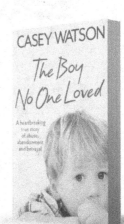

TITLES AVAILABLE AS E-BOOK ONLY

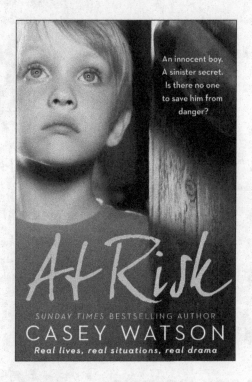

AT RISK

Adam is brought to Casey while his mum
recovers in hospital – just for a few days

But a chance discovery reveals that Casey has stumbled upon
something altogether more sinister . . .

THE LITTLE PRINCESS

Six-year-old Darby is naturally distressed at being removed from her parents just before Christmas

And when the shocking and sickening reason is revealed, a Happy New Year seems an impossible dream as well . . .

DADDY'S BOY

Paulie, just five, is a boy out of control – or is he just misunderstood?

The plan for Paulie is simple: get him back home with his family. But perhaps 'home' isn't the best place for him . . .

THE WILD CHILD

Angry and hurting, eight-year-old Connor is from a broken home

As streetwise as they come, he's determined to cause trouble. But Casey is convinced there is a frightened child beneath the swagger.

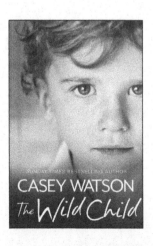

NO PLACE FOR NATHAN

Nathan has a sometime alter ego called Jenny, who is the only one who knows the secrets of his disturbed past

But where is Jenny when she is most needed?

SCARLETT'S SECRET

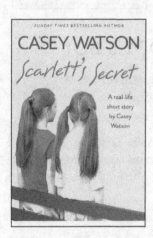

Jade and Scarlett, 17-year-old twins, share a terrible secret

Can Casey help them come to terms with the truth and rediscover their sibling connection?

JUST A BOY

Cameron is a sweet boy who seems happy in his own skin – making him rather different from most of the other children Casey has cared for

But what happens when Cameron disappears? Will Casey's worst fears be realised?

FEEL HEART.
FEEL HOPE.
READ CASEY.

Discover more about Casey Watson.
Visit www.caseywatson.co.uk

Find Casey Watson on 🅕 & 𝕏

MOVING
Memoirs

Stories of hope, courage and
the power of love . . .

Sign up to the Moving Memoirs email and you'll
be the first to hear about new books, discounts,
and get sneak previews from your
favourite authors!

Sign up at

www.moving-memoirs.com